Praise for *Beyond*

'A rich, clear and articulate explanation of a transformative technology.'
    David Spence, former Director and Chairman of PayPal Australia

'Everyone who cares about money is trying to get their heads around DeFi, and what it may mean for financial institutions. This book explains it all, with sparkle, depth and clarity.'
    Michael Jordaan, ex-CEO of First National Bank and co-founder of Bank Zero

'Looking backward to move forward, this book is a masterclass on the evolution and expansion of the crypto world and its possible futures. Essential for those wanting to move beyond the headlines.'
    Herman Singh, Associate Professor, University of Cape Town Graduate School

'The gripping story of the great financial disruption and its portents, told with wit and insight.'
    Ray Hartley, Research Director, The Brenthurst Foundation

Beyond Bitcoin

DECENTRALISED FINANCE AND THE END OF BANKS

Steven Boykey Sidley & Simon Dingle

ICON

Published in the UK and USA in 2022 by
Icon Books Ltd, Omnibus Business Centre,
39–41 North Road, London N7 9DP
email: info@iconbooks.com
www.iconbooks.com

Sold in the UK, Europe and Asia
by Faber & Faber Ltd, Bloomsbury House,
74–77 Great Russell Street,
London WC1B 3DA or their agents

Distributed in the UK, Europe and Asia
by Grantham Book Services, Trent Road, Grantham NG31 7XQ

Distributed in the USA
by Publishers Group West,
1700 Fourth Street, Berkeley, CA 94710

Distributed in Canada by Publishers Group Canada,
76 Stafford Street, Unit 300
Toronto, Ontario M6J 2S1

Distributed in Australia and New Zealand
by Allen & Unwin Pty Ltd, PO Box 8500,
83 Alexander Street, Crows Nest, NSW 2065

Distributed in South Africa
by Jonathan Ball, Office B4, The District,
41 Sir Lowry Road, Woodstock 7925

Distributed in India by Penguin Books India,
7th Floor, Infinity Tower – C, DLF Cyber City, Gurgaon 122002, Haryana

ISBN: 978-178578-830-7

Typeset in Minion by Marie Doherty

Printed and bound in Great Britain by Clays Ltd, Elcograf S.p.A.

CONTENTS

ABOUT THE AUTHORS

Steven Boykey Sidley has worked extensively in technology and finance and is an award-winning novelist, playwright and columnist. An American citizen, he currently lives in Johannesburg. *Beyond Bitcoin* is his sixth book.

Simon Dingle is an author, broadcaster and entrepreneur with extensive experience in cryptocurrency. He has been on the founding teams of several fintech firms, including cryptocurrency exchange Luno and open banking provider Curve.

Disclaimer

The contents of this book do not constitute professional financial advice. Neither the authors nor the publisher shall be liable or responsible for any loss or damage allegedly arising from any information or suggestion contained in this book.

You never change things by fighting the existing reality. To change something, build a new model that makes the existing model obsolete.

Richard Buckminster Fuller

ACKNOWLEDGEMENTS

Along the winding path from conception to publication several people kindly read all or sections of this book, offering encouragement, correction, clarifications, ballast and lifebelts. These include Andre Cronje, Hugh Karp, Michael Jordaan, Eugene Ashton, Ray Hartley, Herman Singh, David Spence, Dr Robin Petersen, Bronwyn Williams, Kate Sidley, Vicki Sidley, Jamie Carr, Rian Malan, our editor Duncan Heath and the rest of the team from Icon Books.

There are also those who had no direct role in shaping our manuscript, but upon whose expertise and insight we gorged – their books, websites, blogs, podcasts, YouTube videos and Twitter feeds. These include Camila Russo, Laura Shin, Nic Carter, Caitlin Long, Nik Bhatia, Lyn Alden, Coinmonks.com, Coindesk.com, Defipulse.com, Coinmarketcap.com, the Lex Fridman podcast, The Defiant podcast, The Fintech Blueprint podcast, Uncommon Core podcast, among countless other sources that informed us along the way. Thank you by proxy.

TIMELINE OF MAJOR EVENTS DISCUSSED IN THESE PAGES

2008	Birth of Bitcoin – Satoshi Nakamoto white paper
2009	First Bitcoin transaction on network
2010	First Bitcoin transaction with real monetary value – two pizzas
2012	Vitalik Buterin co-founds *Bitcoin Magazine*
2013	Ethereum white paper published by Vitalik Buterin
2013	Satoshi drops from sight
2013	First ICO – MasterCoin
2014	Tether stablecoin
2014	MakerDAO and the DAI stablecoin
2015	Ethereum launches
2016	The DAO hack
2017	Chainlink launches
2017	Nexus Mutual launches
2017	'Dragon' CryptoKitty sells for $170,000
2017	SEC files case against Munchee ICO
2018	MakerDAO MKR governance token launch
2018	Compound launches with VC funding
2018	Uniswap V1 launches
2018	Synthetix launches
2018	NFTs protocol ERC-721 released
2018	The word 'DeFi' appears in a Telegram message

2019	Facebook announces Libra
2020	'The Summer of DeFi' – multiple projects launched
2020	Compound's COMP token launch
2020	iEarn launched (later changed to Yearn)
2021	Beeple sells an NFT-permission digital artwork for $69m
2021	Elon Musk tweets about Dogecoin
2021	Andreessen Horowitz $2.1bn crypto fund launched
2021	Wyoming crypto-friendly legislation
2021	Coinbase IPO
2021	World Economic Forum white paper
2021	China bans mining
2021	50% crypto market price crash and energy concerns
2021	El Salvador announces Bitcoin to become legal currency
2021	Crypto clauses inserted into US Infrastructure Bill
2021	$681m Poly hack

PROLOGUE

Any book that confidently proclaims the redefining and refurbishment of the global financial system and the many industries it supports will rightly attract some scepticism, even derision. But there is much afoot now, small explosions of startling economic innovation, burgeoning revolutions happening in myriad matters of technology and commerce, and sharp-toothed dogs snapping at the heels of the world's global financial institutions.

It is called Decentralised Finance. 'DeFi' is its cutesy but sticky nickname.

A reliable way of assessing the breathless predictions of any new technology's disruptive potential is to look at the presumed losers to see how they are reacting.

We did.

Jamie Dimon, CEO of JPMorgan Chase, one of the largest banks in the world, has warned his shareholders of 'enormous competitive threat' from new financial technologies, including 'serious emerging issues' around 'shadow banks', meaning unregulated lending institutions outside of the banking sector. 'They have to be dealt with quickly,' he says. Bank of America muses publicly about the 'best defense of being disintermediated by DeFi'. The Dutch multinational ING compares DeFi to cloud computing in the 1990s – an interesting new innovation then, and the foundational deployment mechanism of the global Internet now. And most tellingly, more than 80 countries have digital currency projects underway at their central banks, all of them in response to a new technology barely known outside a small tech-savvy clique. From banks to stock exchanges to insurance companies to investment giants, from New York to London to Moscow to Beijing, from the tech giants of Silicon Valley to halls of government power, similar pricklings of concern and anxiety are being heard, and defences are being mounted. No one who is looking to the future can ignore it.

And so we are comfortable in saying the following about the sudden appearance of this new financial technology, now just a few years old:

Great fortunes will be made and lost in its wake. Staid and storied institutions will have to shed warm skins in a painful shudder of reinvention.

It will make the startling trillion-dollar rise of Bitcoin look pedestrian by comparison.

It will disrupt and displace fine and respectable companies, if not entire industries, along with careers and skills.

It will make life easier and fairer and less expensive for the rest of us.

It will affect everyone on earth who has ever had a bank account, a credit card, a debit card, a loan, an insurance policy or a lawyer. To say nothing of investors, artists and traders and anyone who would wish to transact globally without the inertia of inscrutable state and private bureaucracies.

It will reforge the cogs and wheels in the engines of trust.

We will argue in these pages that we are not overstating the case: DeFi's growing hype is justified.

CHAPTER 1

Introduction

Aman in Johannesburg wishes to send his daughter studying in The Netherlands some money to spend on an upcoming long weekend. He decides that R1,000 (about $75) seems about right. He goes to his banking website to transfer the money to his daughter's bank account in Amsterdam. On the site he is confronted with an array of forms and questions that seek to shoehorn his intended gift to his daughter into a set of arcane and opaque requirements.

The man gives up at the point where the system attempts to assign a regulatory code to the transaction. He has been on the site for ten minutes. He does not even get to the point where the transaction might have been approved and where the transaction fee would be revealed. Had he done so he would have found out that it was over 15% of his intended gift.

He then opens an application on his phone, a crypto-wallet called Metamask. He transfers $75-worth of a cryptocurrency called ETH from Metamask to his daughter's crypto-wallet, accessed via an app called MyEtherWallet which she had downloaded the previous week in Amsterdam from her laptop. It takes fifteen seconds to enter the transaction. She receives the funds five minutes later. The *transaction fees are a fraction of what her father's bank would have extracted.*

The man fills out no forms to do this transaction. He does not need an ID. The transaction, although having been viewed by thousands of anonymous computers, will never be tied to the father or the daughter. Unlike the bank transfer, the South African government and Dutch government will not ever identify them as the parties to this transaction, even though they would wish to do so.

It is a private matter between father and daughter.

It is simple. It is fast. It is cheap.

✻

The scenario above is not new. It has been around for a few years, certainly longer than the main subject of this book, DeFi. It is in daily use by millions of people. It is trivial to initiate and conclude.

But buried in this little story is an important matter, the crux really.

It is the matter of trust.

The man wishing to send his daughter a payment had two options. One required a 'man-in-the-middle' and the other did not. In this example, the 'man-in-the-middle' was his bank. Not only was the experience frustrating (although, to be sure, while this example is real, not all bank experiences are this bad), it was also expensive. And in this example, accompanied by a usurious rent extraction, both by the bank and the state.

In the man's second attempt to pay his daughter, there was no one sitting in the middle of the transaction. No institution with employees and forms to fill in. Just a few lines of code of little interest to the man who initiated the transaction, or to his daughter. A transaction fee may have been charged to compensate for the expense of the computing resources which shepherded this transaction to its conclusion. But it was much lower than that of the bank.

Bitcoin arrived as an idea in 2008, launched in 2009, and is the last common ancestor of all that has come after (Bitcoin itself still rules the roost in terms of scale and total value but decreasingly so).* It has spawned many offspring, some spinning off into historical footnotes and others surviving and conquering. It is Darwinian in its unfolding, having evolved in its entirety in a little over a decade, as though in a petri dish. And it has turned out to be antifragile, adapting and surviving over time.

One of the evolutionary lines has resulted in the family of projects and applications collectively called DeFi, which started appearing in 2018. There is a famous August 3rd, 2018 screen grab from Telegram, a chat with early innovators in the field – some people from projects called dYdX, 0x, Set Protocol and Dharma. The names on the chat are Blake and Brendan, but there were others, like Felix Feng from Set, who has related the story and shared the screen grab. Names for their new passion were bandied about. OFD – Open Financial Protocols. DFD – Decentralised Finance Developers. Open Lattice, Open Horizon. And then 'DeFi'. I like it, says Blake, it comes out as 'Defy'. And that was it.

And therein lies the core of this book, DeFi. We will describe a big idea, its implications still evolving and ill-understood, and its commercial instantiations appearing daily, not only in finance (where we will spend most of our time) but across myriad other human endeavours.

---

* For the uninitiated, we describe how cryptocurrency and blockchain actually work at various points in the following pages.

This idea had its roots in maths first, and then cryptography, and then the aspiration of a few techno-zealots to build a new financial system, a better one than had existed for centuries.

It was an idea that fed off the perhaps cynical view that the world would be a better place if we trusted no one. Or, rather, that we didn't have to trust humans, institutions and governments, but rather mathematics and logic, protected against politics, change or misinterpretation.

We will describe a set of technological and commercial developments which are, by design and with brutal precision, targeting industries that outsource trust – banks, insurance companies, exchanges and brokers and other trustees across numerous other industries, whose fees are estimated to consume 6% of global GDP, to say nothing of the profits which some of them accrue beyond the selling of trust.

We will briefly and lightly explain the underlying mathematics, and point out the organisations, projects, individuals and services that together comprise this new industry, and we will show exactly where their collective arrows are likely to find their marks in the financial world.

DeFi is coming. Quietly at first. Tentatively at first. Softly at first. And then not.

CHAPTER 2

A matter of trust

Before launching into the Wild West of blockchain and smart contracts and DeFi and banks and metamorphosing financial landscapes, it's worth taking a short look at trust and the role it has played, not so much in financial matters, but everywhere.

It could be argued that human beings start their lives with a surfeit of trust, giving themselves over completely to the protective embrace of their mothers. We have been taught to trust those in our immediate proximity, and authorities. Trust your family, trust the tribe, trust the police. Automatically distrust strangers. And if one has a darker view of nature, one can argue that the older we get, the more our trust in the world leaches away until it is exhausted.

Perhaps that is partly true, or a matter of degree. What is certainly true is that in human interaction, from business to politics to language to the entanglements of intimate relationships, trust is the lifebelt which seems to keep us afloat. Where we find a lack of it, often through bitter experience, we try to take action to enforce it. Contracts. Promises. Threats. Shame. Laws. Police.

Trust inhabits how we operate in the world, from our families and loved ones and friendship circles where layers of trust are assumed, to delegated representatives and authorities in politics and institutions (where trust never seems to last for very long), and on to the wider and unknown world in which we require a little more assurance, and sometimes a lot more. In the circumstances that we address in this book, we find that the best strategy is to have no trust at all.

Google fairly bristles on this topic. Scholarly articles go on for many pages and across decades. This is a big subject, well-trodden, continuously debated, worried over and analysed.

There is one analysis that caught our eye, from a paper entitled 'Information, Irrationality, and the Evolution of Trust' by Manapat, Nowak and Rand, from ScienceDirect.com. The authors discuss trust in the field of investing. They talk about the context of trust evolving under the influence of two important questions. One is knowledge of the trustees. And the other is whether the trustees are in an environment where they need to compete for investors' trust. We will see this directly affecting the matters discussed in this book. The financial organisations that we trust with our valuables are increasingly unknown to us – their brand may be known, so might the employees with whom we interact, but not the inner workings of the products they sell to us, the machines into which our funds are thrown. And they are increasingly monopolistic, not because there are no competitors, but because there is inherent friction in moving from one to another. Anyone serviced by multiple products at one bank, like a savings account, current account, credit cards and a mortgage would balk at restarting with a new bank.

This brings us to one of the core pillars of DeFi, that of *trust-lessness*, a term bandied about since before the birth of Bitcoin. And the other piece of related jargon, *decentralisation*, often ill-understood.

A simple explanation then.

A *trustless* economic system means that participants need not trust anyone in that system. Not even a little. Not the people who built it, not the people who use it, not the people who abuse it. This is true of most of the DeFi projects we will discuss. Trustless architectures are designed around assumption of the worst-case scenario (i.e. everyone is equally liable to be dishonest). You do not even need to trust the system itself.

This is achieved in more than one way. The first is to use maths to ensure immutability in the data stored on the system. It cannot be changed, ever. Not by people and not by malware. It is locked down by mathematics. We will learn a little bit about how that is achieved in the next chapter.

The other is through the mechanism of the *decentralised* system.

A story is illustrative here. There is a small undiscovered island somewhere in the Pacific, with no access to the outside world. There are, say, 150 families on this island. They all reside in the only village, and live bountiful lives, eating coconuts from palm trees and getting shade from their leaves. Each family has one tree. One day, a storm comes over the island and lightning strikes, destroying the tree of the Wok family. That night a meeting is called. Wok's neighbour, the head of the Kek family, says: 'No worries, Wok, I'll lend you leaves and coconuts, and when your tree grows back you can repay me.' So two years later, the tree is back. Kek comes to Wok and says: 'Dude, it's payback time.' Wok says innocently: 'What are you talking about? I don't owe you anything.' A meeting is called. Kek asks: 'Who heard Wok promise to repay me?' 149 families raise their hands (not the Woks, of course); they all heard the same thing. Wok has to pay. The same promise was heard by everyone. It cannot be refuted. Because the transaction was ... decentralised.

This is how decentralisation works in the here and now, only better (imagine if everyone hated Kek because he was a meanie – it could have gone the other way). In the case of cryptocurrencies such as Bitcoin and Ethereum the same transaction can be viewed and checked by hundreds, thousands, even tens of thousands of *anonymous* computers, the operators and owners of which are all unknown to each other. There is always consensus as to what is happening on the blockchain (which is the underlying technology plumbing – the database on which all transactions live for ever, embedded, immutable, auditable and connected in a long chain of data 'blocks'). It is the consensus of strangers, which is the safest kind, even better than 150 families in an island village.

Moreover, what the technology has provided is *scale*. Many small tribal units originally had decentralised decision mechanisms, because there were few enough participants to be manageable, as in our example. But as humans collected in larger and larger groups, this became impractical and led to other forms of decision-making. Decentralised blockchain has brought back the power of the tribal unit, but at scale.

There is one other word associated with this new technology. It is *permissionless*. This means that anyone can participate without asking anyone's permission. There is no one to apply to, and the technology does not know or care who the participants are. Again, this concept is unheard of in TradFi (traditional finance). There is *always* an application form to be accepted or rejected by people or machines behind closed doors. To take a loan. To open an account. To take out insurance. To wire money to another country.

We do not intend to go too deeply into the technical details that ensure trustlessness and decentralisation; they are beyond the scope of our interest, but the concepts are not.

Trustlessness and decentralisation and permissionlessness. The opposite of the world of financial institutions.

(A side note: not all blockchains are decentralised, or permissionless, or trustless, depending on how they are deployed. But the ones we will be considering in this book are.)

CHAPTER 3

Ethereum and the rise of the smart contract

I n trying to determine how we got here and what the ingredients of history were that led to this moment, we immediately are faced with the problem of how far back to cast our gaze. The history of financial institutions is important, and we will get there later. So is Bitcoin, the kindling that combusted in 2009 and started the entire blockchain industry. But there is another starting point that is often overlooked.

It is the invention of a security methodology called public key cryptography, a piece of magic fuelled by a mathematical oddity – the one-way function. Fear not, the following two paragraphs will be about the only reference to maths you will find in this book.

Those of you with any memory of high school will remember the 'function'. One of the first ones you might have learned was $f(x) = x^2$. If you know what is on the left of the equal sign (the value of x), you can calculate what is on the right (the value of x^2). If you know what is on the right side of the equal sign (x^2), you can work out the value of x. This is a two-way function. Two-way functions rule the mathematical roost; they are ubiquitous.

In 1904 a German mathematician named Ernst Zermelo was fiddling with the works of the seminal 19th-century German set theoretician, mathematician Georg Cantor. He noticed that Cantor's work contained certain paradoxes, which eventually gave rise to a class of surprising functions where it was easy to move in one direction, but not the other. These functions are sometimes referred to by mathematicians as trapdoor functions.

Easy to compute one way, very hard to do the reverse. This is the cellular DNA of blockchain technology and indeed of most digital security.

We now jump forward through decades of formal mathematics to 1976. Three cryptographers, Whitfield Diffie, Martin Hellman and Ralph Merkle, had been working for some time on a fiendishly complex problem that can be illuminated by a simple example.

Let's say I have a secret which I write down on a piece of paper, and I lock it in a metal lockbox with my little brass key. If I give you the lockbox, and I later want to give you permission to read my secret, then you must have an identical key to open the lockbox (or I must give you mine). There is no other way.

Diffie, Hellman and Merkle wanted to achieve a way of sharing secrets *without* having to share keys. It was the unsolved problem called the asymmetric key problem, and we will soon see why it was so important.

Diffie and Hellman finally cracked the problem with layers of arcane mathematics, with assistance from Merkle. Diffie and Hellman authored an iconic 1976 paper entitled 'New Directions in Cryptography'. The solution came to be known as the Diffie–Hellman key exchange, and Merkle's name was added in 2002 to recognise his contribution (Merkle also found his own glory elsewhere in cryptography).

There is a fascinating side story around this, described in detail by Simon Singh in his book *The Code Book*. It seems that the British had solved this problem many years earlier in work that was carried out by their intelligence services. It was embargoed under the Official Secrets Act. That they had already cracked this nut only became known to the public when the embargo ended, well after Diffie–Hellman's paper, and too late for the multi-billion-dollar security industry that arose in its wake.

The 1976 Diffie–Hellman–Merkle key exchange was picked up and further developed by three academics – Ron Rivest, Adi Shamir and Leonard Adelman – who developed the RSA algorithm the following year. And eventually and perhaps inevitably, RSA became the foundation of Internet security. (The little yellow lock in your browser window, and the 's' in 'https', means your browser session is secured by cryptography based on the RSA algorithm; meaning that you likely use public key cryptography every day.)

Now we are going to leapfrog a library's-worth of additional maths and computer science and get to the core of the matter – how this all fits into blockchain and cryptocurrency.

You will have heard, incessantly perhaps, about the security of blockchains (both Bitcoin and Ethereum, and others), their unhackability, about the safety of your 'tokens' (cryptocurrency coins) on those blockchains. This is because it is easy for tokens to be deposited by anyone to your wallet address on the blockchain (your 'account' is the easiest way to think of it), but impossible (actually 'too hard' is a better description) for anyone to move tokens out of your account, except you. Using your own private key. Not the little brass one of course, but a string of numbers known only to you. Other people who want to get into your account to make deposits are given another key, called a public key, and they all use the same one. But they can't make withdrawals – for that they need the private key. The whole system uses the one-way function as its logical core.

Easy one way, hard the other. What RSA had done was to give programmatic life to the magic of the one-way algorithm, and in doing so, created the most secure digital key in digital security history.

A side-note: what do we mean when we say that a function is 'hard' to reverse in our world of blockchain and wallets and keys? Go on Google and ask the question 'How long does it take to crack a private key?' You will be assaulted by maths and long debates about assumptions. Here is a good one: if a modern supercomputer had been running since the Big Bang, it still wouldn't have cracked your private key.

This one is even better (and longer):

317,000,000,000,000,000,000,000,000,000,000,000,000,000,
000,000,000,000,000,000,000,000,000,000,000,000,000,000,
000 years.

A long time, then.

Bitcoin

It is not possible to discuss DeFi without discussing Bitcoin. It is the OG, the Original Gangster, of this entire enterprise. But so much has been written, mythologised, recorded, argued and analysed over Bitcoin's short lifetime that we intend only to discuss the sections that illuminate the road to DeFi.

Satoshi Nakamoto's seminal 2008 white paper 'Bitcoin: A Peer-to-Peer Electronic Cash System' birthed the development of the Bitcoin blockchain by a small band of crypto-enthusiasts, including Satoshi, who dropped from sight in 2013. Nobody had ever met him or has since been able to trace him. (It was likely a him, and not a her or a group of people; there is apparently evidence of this in the email trails. Satoshi is also a male name in Japan.)

It was a cool experiment at the beginning, not much more. Its pieces included a type of secure database (now known as a blockchain) that stored tokens called Bitcoins in one of many 'wallets', each wallet simply being an address in the blockchain database. Tokens could be moved around the database from one address to another under instruction by the wallet holder. Anyone could make a deposit to the wallet.

The white paper and its software's expression in the blockchain sought to address multiple problems that existed in real-world money. One of the most important was that of 'double spending', which had bedevilled digital money development from the 1970s when people started toying with the idea. Because digital items are easy to copy, how could people be stopped from copying a digital coin and spending it more than once? The paper solved a host of other issues as well, from security to immutability of transactions history, to the building of ramparts against coordinated network attacks, to democratic open access, to a locked-in resistance against the unrestrained and inflationary printing of new money (this is what governments and their banking proxies have done for millennia, including now via the euphemistically named 'quantitative easing' (QE), a fancy word for government creation of money out of thin air, for example to fund a pandemic response). Satoshi's nine-page document described an entire end-to-end monetary system, from the creation of money to the way it is held, exchanged and transmitted, secured by cryptography, inflation-proof, with no owner, no custodian, no geographic borders, its rules set in stone and impervious to whim or malice. It was, in short, a work of art.

There is some evidence that the original contributors to the project hoped that it would be more than just a fascinating experiment, having created many digital coins for themselves along the way through a process called mining – the ingenious mechanism invented by Satoshi to mint Bitcoins, which we will revisit later in the book. But until the infamous first person (Laszlo Hanyecz) ascribed a first value to a Bitcoin, it was just an interesting project. That first transaction-of-value was 10,000 Bitcoins (BTC) for two pizzas worth $78, sold by the pizza restaurant-owning father of one of the first contributors to the project. The pizza restaurant is Papa Johns and the date of that transaction (May 22nd, 2010) is celebrated by Bitcoin enthusiasts every year. It is called Bitcoin Pizza Day.

And then it took off, almost without pause, driving the fastest and largest movement of value from traditional assets into a new asset in recorded history.

Which leads to an observation and a question – DeFi has not blossomed on the Bitcoin blockchain, because it has taken root elsewhere. Why not?

The Bitcoin blockchain was designed for a single use-case – a system to allow the safe and private storage and transmission of digital money from one digital wallet to another. Purists will demand a little more, so: it is a cryptographically secure database for a token called Bitcoin, supported by an ecosystem consisting of miners (who create Bitcoin) and validators (who validate the integrity of transactions) and the rest of us, wallet owners, all working in a close-knit ecosystem to transact within the Bitcoin monetary system described in Satoshi's white paper. Meaning that there are three actors on the Bitcoin blockchain – those who verify transactions and mint Bitcoins (miners), those who check their work (node validators, thousands of them, many of them running on inexpensive off-the-shelf machines), and the rest of us, who merely store and use our Bitcoin.

Nothing else was envisaged. A single coin – Bitcoin. A single use – creating, storing and transacting Bitcoin. A closed system. Not a fertile place for new-fangled ideas like DeFi to take root (although Bitcoin did provide some facility for additional frills to be created). One could argue that its unwavering focus on one thing drove its success – its acceptance, its hardiness and its now-trusted brand. There are now emerging new technologies to bring DeFi to Bitcoin, but it is too early to say whether they will amount to anything.

We will come back to Bitcoin from time to time, but we now move on to the other dominant global blockchain, Ethereum, and the big idea that has been enabled and fuelled by DeFi – the smart contract.

Ethereum

Like Bitcoin, the history of Ethereum is steeped in lore. Just as Bitcoin was largely the brainchild of Satoshi Nakamoto (even though he credited the work of a number of predecessors on whom his ecosystem had fed, including Nick Szabo, Adam Back and Wei Dai between 1998 and 2005), so too does Ethereum have a godhead. With full cognisance of the many early developers, talented hobbyists and visionaries who put their shoulder to the wheel in the development of Ethereum, the main founding energy behind it belonged to a bone-skinny Russian-Canadian teenager, Vitalik Buterin, who remains the spiritual driving force behind the project.

Ethereum was launched in 2015, a full six years after Bitcoin. Buterin had been a precocious mathematical whizz at school, a teenage videogame nerd, and had become deeply obsessed with Bitcoin, even co-founding one of the earliest magazines in 2012, called *Bitcoin Magazine*. It is amusing to understand how deep in the dark ages this was – it was the era of printed magazines.

There is a story he tells of a sort of Damascene conversion to the basic political tenets of cryptocurrency when he was a teenage gaming nerd. He said in an interview: 'I happily played *World of Warcraft* during 2007–2010, but one day Blizzard removed the damage component from my beloved warlock's Siphon Life spell. I cried myself to sleep, and on that day I realized what horrors centralized services can bring.'

Philosophical gaming epiphanies aside, Buterin wrote the Ethereum white paper in 2013. It presented a big new idea, one which was, from a philosophical standpoint, wildly different from Satoshi's white paper. Instead of a single-use architecture, Ethereum would allow anyone to dream up any financial application and program it to run on the blockchain. (It should be noted that white papers have become de rigueur in new crypto projects; entrepreneurs would never get traction without one. 'Yellow papers' are generally the next document – the implementation and economic details. And 'lite papers' are the dummy's guide to the project.)

Buterin's key principle was that no one person, or even a collection of people, could foresee all of the different ways in which the platform could be used. The original Bitcoin blockchain was designed as a single-use peer-to-peer currency application, and it was never intended that it should be allowed to be used as a Swiss army knife (by the way, it is endlessly confusing to some that the cryptocurrency and the blockchain have the same name – Bitcoin).

But Buterin believed differently.

And so he built what is known as a 'Turing-complete' programming language called Solidity and bound it tightly and immutably to the Ethereum blockchain. This fancy name, 'Turing-complete' (after the great British mathematician Alan Turing), meant that the language was able to solve any computational problem you could throw at it using its native language commands. It could not simply refuse to execute a program, or give up in the middle, or make a mistake.

So, a programming language then. You may have heard of C or Python or JavaScript. This language was similar in dialect but simpler, more compact. Developers could learn how to use it in days. The language provides a bunch of pre-written functions for often-used tools, ones you might expect in a language that was to be used in finance and money, like *withdraw* or *spend* or *balance*. And the ability to specify 'if-then-else' rules, which allows contract conditions to be coded. The resulting programs in the world of Ethereum are called 'smart contracts': programs, smallish ones, each expressing a set of rules, exceptions, inputs and outputs (specifically the conditions under which value moves from one wallet address to another). And the contracts are visible to all, and secured by the same mathematical provability for which cryptography is well known. Just like a real-world contract, but immutable, provable and transparent.

Lex Fridman is a podcaster who invites very big thinkers from many disciplines onto his show and shoots the breeze for a couple of hours. He has had physicists, politicians, philosophers, social scientists, computer scientists, and plenty of crypto entrepreneurs and commentators. On one podcast with DeFi luminary Sergey Nazarov (CEO of a DeFi project called Chainlink) he spends some time on the deeper meaning of the smart contract.

He makes the larger point that civilisation has been built on the rails of interactions between humans, and the language that is used between them. Language is interpretive and occasionally ambiguous; so we sometimes fail to achieve perfect human communication. Fridman points out that books have been written on the interpretation of single sentences (and sometimes words) on which matters of great import have hinged. There are circumstances where ambiguity is the enemy, such as when two entities need to agree on some set of facts, conditions and outcomes. And one of the tools we use as a civilisation is the contract, drawn up by experts like lawyers. Even then there is sometimes imperfect communication, which is why we have courts to adjudicate.

Computer languages, by design, are just the opposite. They are entirely deterministic. No book will ever be written about a line of code, as Fridman points out. A piece of code cannot be ambiguous or misinterpreted.

The genius of the smart contract, imagined and implemented by the original Ethereum team, is that it is designed to merge human agreements (specifically financial agreements) into a formal computer language, made unambiguous and deterministic. The 'smart' contract that is implemented is not only open for all to see, it is also secured by cryptography, 100% resistant to change.

In the world of traditional finance, contracts between humans and the financial institution are often too complex for most of us to understand, perhaps purposely so (there is a reason for fine print). They are also often opaque, dense and able to be changed at the whim of the more powerful party (who hasn't received an unbidden fee increase email? To whom does one complain?). Financial institution contracts are drawn up by expensive lawyers. Signatories on the other side, you and I, rarely have the opportunity or resources to have an independent lawyer weigh in on their fairness, and even if we did, the balance of power dictates that the institution will not change a thing. So we generally just sign. Mostly we don't even read the contract.

Smart contracts on Ethereum stand in stark contrast to this. Anyone can see the code. Its decentralised and open nature means that many do. The wisdom of crowds weighs in on the contract's integrity and fairness.

It is, in the words of Fridman, a transformative idea.

And so our story starts here, with a blockchain called Ethereum and a smart contract programming language called Solidity and enough time since its 2015 launch to have gained the trust of developers and libertarians and visionaries and some chancers, all hoping to pull down the mighty edifices of the financial world. And more.

But first. What is a bank?

CHAPTER 4

Financial institutions - targets on their backs

This book is subtitled 'The End of Banks'. This is an exaggeration – it really means the end of banks as we know them. Banks and other financial institutions will have to wrench themselves out of the comfort of the past, where innovation has been slow and the money has been easy and the computers whirr quietly in large data centres. Some will and some others, we predict, will not make it. There is a train coming at these companies, fuelled by blockchain and the invention of the smart contract.

Very few services offered by these companies in their present form can survive, particularly given the massive supporting infrastructure required. A large slice of the TradFi industry will be shown up by DeFi as slow, inflexible, expensive, unfair, opaque and inefficient. This chapter will summarise some of the obvious vulnerabilities in these institutions. For each one discussed briefly here, further detail will be foraged in subsequent chapters.

One of the early DeFi pioneers, Rune Christensen, makes the point that DeFi was saturated with arrogance early on, thinking that millennia's-worth of financial institutional design had been built by fools. Of course, this isn't the case. The problems which DeFi entrepreneurs face have been faced by traditional finance since the beginning. How much to charge for loans, how much to pay for deposits, how to clear and settle, how to calculate risk, etc. DeFi pioneers were not the first people to grapple with this. But we shall see how the new tools enabled by decentralised trustless architectures and blockchain are allowing the construction of an entirely new financial edifice.

Taking a deep dive into the history of banking and how it started and who its stakeholders were and how it evolved is a vertiginous experience. Banks have had a commanding role in the development of civilisation; they have both mirrored and fuelled humanity's progress. Let's ignore central banks for now, those entities tasked by governments with national monetary hygiene, and let's ignore the development of money – we will get back to these later.

Long ago, well before the common era, there were what is generally called proto-banks. Often these were connected to farming and food, like storage and grain loans used by farmers. Proto-banks eventually evolved, under the pressure of urbanisation, with the growth of business, with the spread of literacy, with the requirements of both cross-country trade and war (both ravenous consumers of capital).

There is no general agreement about when 'modern' banking started. Some of the literature references the Medicis in Italy in the 1300s, others will point to later incarnations in England or Spain or Holland or earlier banks elsewhere, including Sumeria, Greece, Egypt, China, the Roman Empire. There is even an inscribed physical tablet called The Code of Hammurabi dating to about 1750 BCE from ancient Babylonia which describes interest-bearing loans.

Pinning the date of establishment of the first modern bank (or even defining a modern bank) is a matter for financial historians to debate. But there are interesting matters along the way which end up with the marbled downtown behemoth that now has your trust.

The first two fundamental services of the modern bank were, and still are, the custodianship of valuables and the extending of loans or credit. The latter of these was constrained in the early banks, like today, by the creditworthiness of the borrower. This may have been determined by status (like noblemen), or wealth, or the standing of the guarantor (the king standing surety for loans to armies, for instance). Loans became simpler matters when tied to collateral, whether it be land or the temporary stewardship of humans or animals or any other items of value, like gold jewellery. Or the certainty of future cash flow to service the debt. Central to this loan exercise is a document of some kind, variously called commercial paper, letters of credit, a mortgage, a credit card contract or any other mutual accord between lender and borrower, recording amount, term and other conditions.

The other core service was the bank offering itself as a trusted depository. This once meant valuables – coins, weapons, jewels. And a receipt of deposit, either paper-based or, in some cases, given on verbal trust. Early banks were trusted not only to return the depositors' value on demand, but to guard it against theft, just as they are today.

It would be tempting to say that the modern 21st-century bank is the same, save for detail. But it is not accurate. New services have appeared and taken wing (payment services, insurance products, brokerage and trading, risk services, foreign exchange services, credit card issuance, ATM access, derivatives). These services (and others) on offer by most large financial institutions are a long way from the two core services of loan and deposit pioneered by the founding modern banks. All of the above are prime targets for the myriad DeFi projects rolling off the production line, cumulatively having attracted over $200 billion in capital at the time of writing. This is negligible when compared to the trillions locked up in the global banking system ($130 trillion, by one measure, nearly twice the global GDP). But that system is, conservatively, about one thousand years old, and DeFi arrived a blink of an eye ago.

Which brings us back again to the matter of trust.

It is sometimes a shock to walk into a large city bank and be assailed by the no-expense-spared lobby, the high-value art works and ostentatious furniture and rich fittings. Surely, we think, they could have saved the many millions paid for, at least partly, by us? Surely they could have built in a cheaper part of town, replaced the marble with a more prudent substitute?

Of course, the reason is obvious. The broadcasting of wealth and taste is seen as an indicator of quality and wisdom and business acumen. You can trust us, the Doric columns and lobby fountain and free cappuccino bar proclaim – just see how well we've done.

Trust us. How is that defined?

Here's a handy list of things the banks would like to sell under the trust message. We won't lose your deposits. If you need help buying that house we've got the capital. We'll never go out of business. We understand the complex mathematics of risk, and would never expose your money to it. We give you the best deal. We are the best guardians of capital. We have every service under our roof, for any of your money needs. We'll respond quickly and personally to you. We'll navigate the regulatory waters so you don't have to. We've been around for ever, we know the ropes. We'll make your money grow.

All of these and more presumably wend their way into any bank's brief to their advertising partners, sooner or later. Without this sale, nobody buys the product. Trust is at the centre of it.

Yes, well.

It is true, for the most part, that you can trust your bank to do what it says it's going to do. Won't lose your deposits, will evaluate risk, will loan you money, make sure it's all legal, abide by the contracts that you were unlikely to have read.

But you won't get the best deal.

Because you pay for that trust. Through fees, sub-optimal interest rates, high-priced loans, inefficient old IT systems, too many employees, executive perks, expense accounts and, of course, helping to maximise the profits of the bank. A bank may argue that its trust is earned. A more sober view is that we bought that trust, and we are paying too much.

One might argue that the high-overhead main street bank is reaching end of life, courtesy of the burgeoning financial technology (fintech) industry and the rise of 'neobanks' – those new entrants powered by the Internet, cloud delivery and deregulation, at least in some countries like the UK. Some of the legacy banks' buildings might be sold or the leases allowed to expire, the marble stripped and employees let go as the services retreat behind mobile phones and PCs, exemplified by new digital-only banks like Revolut and Allica and Bella. This is fair comment; costs will be lowered, but only to the floor of what is possible in a legacy system where certain matters are cast in stone – interbank rates, settlement and clearing costs, central bank policies, SWIFT, various fossilised transaction fees and onerous compliance requirements.

There is a second matter which is largely overlooked by most people, and it is that financial institutions do not treat all of their customers equally. Everyone is ranked according to how much profit can be extracted from them and treated on a sliding scale of attention. If you think this is not true, consider what you are offered when you have a total of $200 to open a new account, compared to a multi-billion-dollar company that wishes to switch its business to a new bank. Which one will get a better interest rate? Which one will be taken out for dinner? If you are rich, you are a more import-ant customer to the bank. It is so obvious as to be tautological, and no one even thinks about it. But we would argue that it's not fair, and it doesn't have to be that way. The playing field is not level.

And then there is the third and not inconsiderable matter of lock-in. Moving from one bank to another is comparable to moving home. Lots of boxes to tick, lots of anxiety and lots of uncertainty about whether the decision will make you happier. Most people don't bother, they just grin and bear their current banking part-ner, even if they are faced with spotty service, long call-centre times, crappy interfaces and sometimes mistakes that never get rectified. Worse, the next bank chosen usually offers much the same thing. Same products, same rates, same showy promises of trust rewarded. Even in those jurisdictions where regulators have insisted on ease of migration, like the UK, it still hardly seems worth the effort.

A final observation. Institutions like banks are not the only guardians of pools of capital. In fact, they have a declining share. Others, like large hedge funds and other investment structures, are now in charge of significant amounts of capital, and they fall outside of at least some of the banking regulatory net. These com-panies are making inroads into previously bank-only services like loans. DeFi will be there too, and may find surprising collaborators in that sector, less encumbered as they are by legacy and regulation.

So let's trawl through some of the services we find at a modern bank, and expose their weaknesses.

Deposits and loans

At the end of the month (or more frequently) most of us, if we care to, will glance at our bank statements, which, among other things, may include savings deposits, money market investments, current accounts and other deposit products, where you entrust the bank with your funds.

At the bottom of these reports, particularly for transacting accounts like current accounts, there might be a fixed transaction account fee applied. We agreed to this transaction fee when we opened the account. It was embedded in some likely inscrutable contract which we signed without reading properly. If we had to ask, please explain how this fee is calculated, what its rationale is, we would not get very far. That is not for us to know. We do know that they have our funds. We do know that they are paying a lower interest rate than they are receiving when they loan those funds out. And yet there is an added transaction fee. Why?

The size of the interest rate we are offered is either fixed, or floats against some external data peg. Generally, the longer the term you agree not to withdraw your funds, the better the rate. Why are we getting a lower rate for liquid accounts? Again, please explain why this is, show us the actual algorithm, the actuarial calculations. You will never get to see it, because it is assumed to be bank intellectual property. Not for our eyes. Opacity is the financial institution's friend.

There are a number of DeFi projects which compete in the deposit/yield space. One of the best known of these is Yearn, which we will discuss in detail later. What Yearn does (at least in its initial

Version 1; later versions have become more sophisticated) is to look across the DeFi space for other projects that require crypto capital, usually for lending or trading or other uses, and that are paying interest to attract that capital. Yearn sniffs around to find the best deal, and you, the depositor, get the best interest available at that time, until Yearn finds a better deal. This new service is called 'yield farming' and is not remotely possible in the traditional financial world. Because of lock-in and the sludge of administration.

Consider how revolutionary this service is, from a banking perspective:

- Every depositor is treated equally, no matter how much is deposited (not true of banks).
- Depositors' funds are automatically (and continually) moved to the entity providing the highest returns (not true of banks).
- Internal workings of the product are open and transparent and secured by cryptography (not true of banks).
- Depositing capital requires no signature, no ID, no paperwork (not true of banks).
- Time to set up accounts and transfer funds is measured in seconds – there is no account approval process (not true of banks).
- Interest rates are higher than at any commercial bank, sometimes by an order of magnitude, even when risk-adjusted.

How can a bank possibly compete against this? If you were the CEO of a financial institution, might you not be worried about your lunch being eaten?

On the other side of the balance sheet are loans. Banks take clients' deposited funds (and central bank funds, under certain conditions) and loan them out again, at a higher rate than the depositor is paid. The spread between the deposit rate and the loan rate (minus the cost of risk) is one of the largest sources of bank profits. Also, the bank can make loans to the value of up to ten or twenty times the amount it has on deposit, called fractional lending. All legal and under the carefully considered guidelines of many smart global and national industry bodies, but if all or even most depositors pulled their money out at once, the bank would immediately be insolvent. And, as we know, that has happened in many notorious bank runs throughout history.

Of course, there is the issue of how much clients are charged for loans. Behind the scenes, risk managers wrangle statistics to come up with an answer. What's the loan for? How certain are we that the client can repay it? What's an appropriate term of the loan? Is it for a house or a new factory or a new nuclear plant? Is it for a company or individual? Is it for a car? If it is for a company, are future cash flows dependable? Does the currency exchange rate impact the risk? Is the place where the funds will be used politically stable?

These and hundreds of other data points pile up and pile up, get turned into probabilities and spreadsheets and equations, and are eventually returned with a no-thank-you or a smile and a contract. The contract will include lots of unreadable fine print covering things like what happens if you miss even a single payment. Again, you have no access at all to the inner workings of the agreement, its basis, its underlying economics and statistics and whether the decision was made by a machine or an optimistically named 'credit committee'. If you don't like it, go to another lender who will likely use similar maths to make similar decisions. Just don't ask to examine the books. And of course, if you are looking for a small loan, don't expect a dinner invitation from us, or an expenses-paid trip to that resort – that's for the people to whom we loan a billion or more. We also answer their calls on the first ring.

Later on we will take a look in more detail at some of the DeFi lending protocols now attracting customers, like Compound, which was one of the first out of the gate. As with Yearn in yield farming, the world of lending and borrowing has attracted a flurry of startling innovation. These projects deal with exactly the same basic question as the financial institutions – what is my certainty that the loan will be repaid, and under what conditions should this loan be approved? The difference is that the smart contracts that the crypto-lenders have devised to answer these questions are, again, open and transparent and the same for everyone no matter the size of the loan, requiring no middleman, no credit committee, no fancy lobbies and no armies of analysts. Meaning that the rates will be lower and the time to approval faster. The banks won't be able to compete.

There is obviously a question of physical collateral, often used to secure a loan. We will go on to take a deeper look at some of the ideas being developed by the DeFi industry around innovations conjoining digital value collateral and physical collateral, how that can be secured and improved by smart contracts.

Before we leave this summary of banking services being eyed by DeFi, we should mention a critical back-office service that handles massive volumes of value: clearing and settlement. In any transaction between two parties there is a time gap between the initiation of the sale and the conclusion. On the retail side, where consumers may wish to make a payment to another party, it is generally quite short, but on the institutional side, particularly in global capital markets, it is longer. Trading desks may be exchanging hundreds of millions or more on behalf of their clients, risk is high, and there is a large software stack on both sides of the transaction that slowly and determinedly moves the transaction and its associated documentation (like external proof of ownership, if it is a movement of shares, for instance) to conclusion.

These transactions are generally days in duration and sometimes more. Companies like Broadridge are deploying blockchain and smart contracts to compress the maddeningly long process chains to shrink clearing and settlement down from days to minutes and less, which will have dramatic effects on the velocity of capital flow. Companies like these, while part of the greater DeFi community, operate quietly and in the background within traditional finance, not wishing to join the brashness of some of the retail DeFi offerings, and preferring to concentrate on process improvements rather than showier DeFi tools of creating and listing crypto tokens for a variety of uses within a given project.

Deposits and loans sit smugly on the comfortable perch of traditional banks. But DeFi is coming.

Insurance

Insurance, another industry pillar in financial services, has a similar set of opacities, inefficiencies, unfairnesses and indeterminacies that put a DeFi target on its back. To give a few examples, drawn from the similar information asymmetry described in banking above:

- Actuarial wizardry (which calculates risk and cover and premium) is hidden from customers.
- Pay-outs are sometimes contested, because real life is messy, and fault and blame and accident and bad luck are often entangled and multivariate.

- Risk calculations are too broad and too blunt and too non-granular. The driver who has an accident through negligence is different from the driver who crashed because a bee flew up his nose while driving.
- Insurance companies, like banks, host massive infrastructures to support what can be simply captured in lines of code in DeFi smart contracts and these infrastructures are run on thousands of untrusted anonymous computers.
- Customers are often put under a term of contract. A year or more. You can't move until the term is up.
- Like in the bank description, large customers are treated differently than small customers, and the smallest of customers, with few assets, are not that welcome. Tiny premiums are not of interest to most insurers or their brokers, nor can their processes handle it.

Later on we'll look at Nexus Mutual and the new crop of DeFi insurers, and how an entrenched legacy of mega-insurers will start to lose its hold.

Trading and exchanges

Financial institutions often have trading desks, facilitating trades and buying and selling assets on behalf of their customers and sometimes on behalf of themselves. Such assets include stocks, bonds and other debt, government paper, commodities, futures, options. These are sometimes large institutional trades, and sometimes retail trades on behalf of bank customers. In either case the bank will charge for the services, which is usually a fee on top of other fees, because other intermediaries have to be paid along the way to transaction finalisation, such as external exchanges.

Outside of the banking sector there are the public exchanges like the New York Stock Exchange or the London Stock Exchange, and many brokerages in front of those, like Schwab or Interactive Brokers who will execute your trade for a fee. Exchanges are one of the bustling areas of DeFi innovation. TradFi electronic exchanges (they're all electronic now – gone are the days of 'open outcry' where traders literally yelled their orders at brokers) are used to match buyers and sellers and to execute a transaction between them. This is now done, in almost all cases, automatically, with the exchange creating an electronic order book and finding buyers and sellers who most closely match the bid and ask price of the asset being discussed (stock or bond or whatever). When the buyer and seller are close in price, a deal can be made. When they are not, the deal may never happen. When a deal closes, the exchange takes a cut. So we have a willing buyer and a willing seller and a trusted party (or parties) in the middle facilitating the deal and taking a cut. That's the problem. The man-in-the-middle again.

There are other problems with electronic exchanges, even the modern ones that provide smooth digital user experiences, and they have to do with regulation or self-protection. One of the authors has an account with a well-known online exchange. Recently it changed its terms and conditions (the asymmetry of this was brutal; no real reasons were given). A document was made accessible to all account holders: 22 pages of dense legalese and 34 clauses. We are sure everyone is dying to read it. While the exchange may well have had teams of lawyers advising it to do this to protect itself, one has to wonder whether there is a less adversarial and contemptible way to act towards your customers.

The DeFi solution is called a DEX, a decentralised exchange. It means that buyers and sellers can trade directly through the magic of a smart contract under the neutral eyes of lots of anonymous decentralised computers which need not trust each other. No middlemen. No onerous pages of legalese. Just you and some lines of code that finds a willing trader to take your bid or offer.

There are a number of these DEXs out there already operating, facilitating billions in transactions, like Uniswap, which we will be exploring in more detail later, and particularly a DEX innovation called an Automated Market Maker which does away with the need for order books. Right now most DEXs operate in the cryptocurrency space, facilitating exchange of one token for another, a roaring business as people speculate on which token's price will rise and which will fall, or require swaps to cryptocurrencies that facilitate various other conveniences like interaction with TradFi.

But we believe that DEXs are the future of most if not all exchanges, for all the reasons that make DeFi so transformative. They're coming for stocks and bonds and titles and futures and commodities and options soon.

Payments

The facilitation and development of new payment instruments by the financial industry is one area which has seen considerable innovation over the last twenty years. From mobile bank front-ends to QR-initiated transactions to chip-based debit cards with wireless transmitters to digital wallets, payment has seen a flurry of improvements by both financial institutions and third-party partners. China, for instance, has become a society where cash is rare and wallets live in cheap smartphones, spread over an entire population. Almost all payments are digital, whether personal or business.

But here too, there is change coming. Micropayments, for instance, secured by blockchain. Streaming payments, clocked in value per second. Instantaneous secure institutional payment, including cross-border, obviating the need for clearing and settlement. Remittances too – a massive business for people outside of the formal sector and currently saddled with onerous transaction fees, with one country, El Salvador, having welcomed blockchain technology to solve remittance overhead as a government-supported initiative.

Before we close this summary, a sidebar.

Much of what we will discuss in this book will support our hypothesis that financial institutions are soon to be faced with an existential crisis, faster than even the most paranoid of them may believe. But there are a number of related revolutions happening in and around the blockchain space – in ownership certainty, in identity authentication, and in how to integrate data from the external physical world, like commodity prices or weather data. We will touch on some of these too, perhaps only obliquely related to financial institutions, but all adding colour and texture to this generous-sized canvas.

CHAPTER 5

A short note to our banker, our friend

T he authors know a few bankers. Some of them are friends. Personal friends. Contrary to the bashing we may be seen to be giving to an entire industry, the truth is that, like all industries, most bankers are good and honest folk doing their jobs with diligence, and truly caring about their customers. And banks are simply acting within their mandates and in the interests of their shareholders, and within the constraints of their industries.

Many of these people that we know, at least at the time of writing (and somewhat surprisingly, even given our unscientific sample), have never heard of DeFi. But they are aware of a number of things. They are aware that there is a huge IT department in their bank and large computers bearing big brand names doing important things with scary software and lots of programmers, and that requests for changes or features or product improvements are a long, hard, frustrating slog. All are aware that there are really cool developments happening out there in fintech – small, nimble companies doing clever stuff and skimming off traditional bank revenue for themselves. Venmo, PayPal, Revolut and others come to mind.

Most of our banker friends, at least on the customer sales side, have only a vague idea of the details of the products that they sell, and would not expect them to be shared anyway, given their assumed complexity, understood only by the witches and wizards in the dark coven where they are cooked up. It is not their fault, my friends; they are given black boxes to sell.

Our banker friends are intrigued by Bitcoin, by Ethereum. Some have invested in them, and all manner of other wild cryptocurrency gambles. Some of them have made money.

Few of them, however, know what a smart contract is. Or what decentralisation means, or trustlessness, or why it is important.

Few of them know that their jobs might disappear one day.

It is a matter of historical, economic and business interest that these industries have grown very large over hundreds of years (ignoring for now that some outside of finance, like FAANG – the abbreviation given to the juggernaut of Facebook, Apple, Amazon, Netflix and Google – have grown large over only tens of years, and now have started to encroach on financial services). Some banks have grown too large to fail, as we saw in the sub-prime crisis. So large that they are hard to move, inflexible, risk-averse, predictable. The older industries – like banking, insurance, mining, manufacturing, automotive and others – are weighed down by processes and cultures that have grown deep roots over time, anchoring those industries and giving them their institutional memory and stability. New and more efficient technologies may arrive over time, but integration and acceptance within these large structures is plodding and challenged by apathy at every turn. Anyone who has worked in a large corporation will have many of these stories to share.

One of the authors worked as Group Chief Technology Officer for a (then) Fortune 250 company. Simple matters like the approval of a new supplier of even minor goods, or an insubstantial change in a screen interface to make it easier to use, or the adoption of an external cloud-based productivity platform, or even the hiring of a needed new employee were maddening affairs, requiring forms, submissions, rationales, approvals. It is the nature of the beast. Big, lumbering.

Sclerotic.

And so we see the financial institutions, finally, well over a decade after the first movers arrived, rolling out account and payment services on mobile or phasing out chequebooks or allowing remote work or redesigning their user interfaces. Often not very well.

One of the authors was once proudly shown the results of an innovation project at a major bank in which an account holder could check their balance on their Apple Watch. A task that could be written, tested and deployed in under an hour by any vaguely competent developer. Innovation requires a fleetness of foot and a willingness to risk failure. Not part of a bank's lexicon.

DeFi has no such encumbrances; it has started with a clean canvas and a technology palette of astonishing new magic. Banks cannot compete – the best that one can hope is that they collaborate and incorporate. They eventually will have no other choice.

And to our friends in financial institutions – it's not your fault. Your institution moves, well, at institutional speed.

CHAPTER 6

ICO mania - aspirants, chancers and crooks

New ventures are notoriously difficult to fund, as much today as at any point in entrepreneurial history. There is a series of layers of capital available to someone with an idea and some energy, starting with the entrepreneur's own bank account, and then family and friends and colleagues (often called 'angels', amusing in that these friendly funders are often as grim a taskmaster as anyone who comes later). And then up the stack – venture capitalists, Series A, B, C and D investors (each coming in with larger amounts as the company grows) and then, if stars align, a public listing or a buy-out from a bigger company.

Interesting parallel funding channels also compete for good ideas: incubators, accelerators, corporate innovation funds, NGOs and the more recent crowdfunds, enabled by the Internet.

But, as the authors can attest in their own endeavours, finding money to start a company takes thick skin and heroic determination. Moreover, the entrepreneur's idea has to walk a fine line. If the idea is not new, and has been exploited elsewhere, an investor would likely decline, unless there was a clever new angle. If an idea is so new as to be a market slayer (or creator), an investor might wonder why, if the idea was so good, no one else had stepped up. Or worse, the investor may not get it at all, unbelieving as to its potential, blind to its vision.

Which is where the crypto industry found itself, after Bitcoin finally became more than a hackers' project. For the people in the early to mid-2010s who understood where this technology must lead, the commercial potential was so obvious as to be tautological. And adding hurdle to hill, most of these people were young and edgy and largely unschooled in how to dress up an idea for investors in a glass-walled conference room, even those investors for whom eccentric founders were old hat.

So, endless ideas for uses of trustless decentralised permissionless blockchains, and incredulous investors saying WTF. Until the price of Bitcoin took off.

Even then, investors were cautious. Investments in 'shovels' (mines, etc.) rather than 'gold' (the tokens or new blockchain architectures) started to appear in the venture capital (VC) community, but there was little interest in a young person proclaiming that he or she had the next Bitcoin. Those were confident proclamations of moonshots, without too much supporting data or industry history, and so investors remained shy.

So where did the early crypto-entrepreneurs turn to for money? They turned to us. The public. There were plenty of people in those early days prepared to take a punt on an untested cryptocurrency, as long as there was a fancy (and sometimes mathematically inscrutable) white paper to back it up. You didn't need Sand Hill Road in Silicon Valley, where the great VC companies live. You didn't need vast numbers of public investors who had never even heard of Bitcoin. You just needed a few thousand people who were paying attention to the technology. And then, rather quickly, you simply needed a few thousand people who might not know about tech, but who were paying attention to Bitcoin's meteoric price rise, and hoping to get lucky on a new offering. If blockchain technology was to decentralise trust networks, why shouldn't it also decentralise the funding of new projects?

And so the early cryptocurrency hopefuls found a market for capital. They would sell their tokens in the open market. On a website. Believers would snap them up cheap, before they became the next Bitcoin.

And therein lies a story or two.

The Securities and Exchange Commission (SEC) in the US was established on June 6th, 1934. Stock markets had been around since 1531 (Antwerp), 1772 (London) and 1791 (New York). The early stock exchanges in Europe had largely been a mechanism for the great trading companies (like the Dutch East India Company) to finance fleets of ships carrying goods to and from the East. Investors could finance a single fleet consignment (a one-time limited-liability investment), and later could invest in the shares of those companies that had received what were called 'charters' from the government.

It is not a surprise that the history of exchanges was rife with mischief. Companies that lied, companies that hardly existed except for their share certificates, lost deeds of share ownership, price bubbles, inside information, conflicted owners and all manner of grifters looking for easy money.

Along the way, governments tried, to a greater or lesser extent, to protect the naive citizen investor. In the US, for instance, the Blue Sky Laws of 1911 were meant to do exactly that. But they were poorly thought out, poorly implemented and poorly policed. So the crash of 1929 was sort of inevitable. A bubble (fuelled by price manipulators) and a pop, a big one. Ruined lives and livelihoods and all manner of dominos falling, including mass unemployment.

Hence the SEC, eventually enforcing a series of laws to protect investors: the Glass–Steagall Act of 1933, the Securities Exchange Act (1934), the Public Utility Holding Company Act (1935), the Trust Indenture Act (1939), the Investment Advisers Act (1940) and the Investment Company Act (1940).

This time the government was serious. Citizens were not there to have their pockets rifled on public exchanges. People who crossed the SEC could go to jail, and did. Which is why, when a company decides to list on an exchange, there are reams of statutory requirements, including the prospectus which essentially says: here is what we do, here is what we're going to do *and here is why it is a terrible idea to invest your money with us*. Really, reading one of these is vaguely comical. Every risk that every retained lawyer and company executive can dream up is listed in lurid legalese. One dare not over-promise because the SEC has a big stick.

For this reason, when the cryptocurrency aspirants looked to raise money from the public, the question arose – how can we do this without it looking like a public offering of securities?

This question was confounded by the fact that lawyers who really understood the regulatory landscape, and the SEC itself, were unsure of what a crypto token was. A currency? A share? A collectible? A commodity? Property? A coin or token residing on a blockchain, with an uncertain future of price, and sometimes a token of dubious utility (like a 'governance' token widely used today, allowing holders a vote on matters pertaining to the underlying project's future development) represented a puzzle.

What was this strange thing indeed?

One of the first things that lawyers acting on behalf of crypto companies did was to apply a famous set of questions comprising what was called the Howey Test. This was defined in US law via a 1946 Supreme Court decision in a case called *SEC vs Howey* which sought to define what constituted an investment contract. The court said that if the transaction was an investment of money in a *common enterprise* with the *expectation of profit*, *solely* from the *efforts* of management, then it should be considered as an investment contract. There were many fraught words in that stream of legalese: 'common enterprise', 'expectation of profit', 'solely', 'efforts'. Lawyers salivate at the opportunity to interpret and argue imperfect language such as this.

In any event it meant that if a cryptocurrency were to pass the test, then the selling of a crypto token would be considered a security. Meaning all of the protections inherent in an initial public offering would apply, and miscreants could go to jail. Prospectuses and other expensive documents would have to be prepared, and risks would have to be enumerated. Millions in lawyer fees would accrue. Few of these crypto pioneers had that sort of money.

And here everyone ran into the problem of speed. The SEC is a government institution, perhaps the slowest moving of all human enterprises. And what was happening with crypto was at the other end of the scale; moving so fast as to be hard for even the most canny observers to see.

The entrepreneurs dove in quickly, having received only bewildered legal guidance on the matter. The risk was deemed worth it. Followed in fairly short order by chancers who had merely copied blockchain code from open-source repositories and renamed them (Dogecoin, worth over $30bn at the time of writing, was entirely open about this – it was supposed to have been a joke).

Others raised fortunes on dubious and even doomed ideas. It was, as they say, a batshit crazy time. Money was easy, and the regulatory regime set up to protect consumers was unable to respond.

The first ICO (Initial Coin Offering) was MasterCoin in July 2013, raising what was then an extraordinary $600,000 (how quaint, from this perspective) from the sale of its MSC crypto token. It is interesting to note that the blockchain developed at MasterCoin has been successful (and underlies the Tether stablecoin technical ecosystem (see next chapter), one of the largest cryptocurrencies by market capitalisation), whereas the original cryptocurrency coin MSC languishes unloved, untraded and essentially worthless.

Other initiatives followed in quick succession, with amounts raised growing rapidly, and coin sales sometimes sold out in minutes. Chronologically: NextCoin, CounterParty, MaidSafeCoin and Swarm. Taking us to Ethereum, the mother of DeFi. So we slow down for this.

Camila Russo, in her book *The Infinite Machine*, tracks the progression of Ethereum's ICO (and the cast of characters behind it) in riveting detail. There had been considerable anticipation about an Ethereum ICO; everyone knew that it was an important new project. Certainly most crypto players knew about it, and had read the white paper. As had a few in the slowly awakening investment community. Expectations were building.

But Vitalik Buterin was very cautious. He wanted to raise funds without raising the ire of the SEC or anyone else who could later arrive to hamper or shut down the project – or worse, to arrest the executives. So the core Ethereum team set out to enlist advice, to look for loopholes, bulletproof the fund-raise.

No one could give them comfort. Until one attorney, well versed in technology (and a Silicon Valley transplant) had an idea, which has proved from this point in history to have been prescient. His name was Steven Nerayoff. Ethereum's native cryptocurrency is called Ether, its trading name shortened to ETH. Nerayoff had delved into the inner workings of Ethereum and realised that ETH, as well as being a cryptocurrency, was also used to pay participants helping to verify transactions. Transactions are calculated in variable units of ETH called 'gas'. It is a transaction fee, fair payment for services. It meant that ETH had utility other than as a pure profit generator. It was one of the cogs in the machine, not just a price appreciation opportunity. This was a key realisation. It meant the Ethereum Foundation had a defence against the claim that Ether was simply a security.

Nerayoff consulted with Jeffrey Alberts from the prestigious New York law firm Pryor Cashman. Alberts concurred and agreed to have an opinion written on Pryor Cashman letterhead.

It was enough to mitigate Vitalik's concerns. Ethereum launched its ICO on August 31st, 2014. It raised $18.3m over two months. Small by later standards, but perfectly sufficient for their needs. The chassis for thousands of decentralised applications, including DeFi, had been built.

The SEC had still not properly ruled on the legality of this or any other offering. And entrepreneurs (and more salubrious parasites) had become emboldened. The successful Ethereum ICO unleashed the floodgates.

Things got wild. Some ICOs were sold out in minutes. First Blood, a company selling tokens to be used as rewards in video-games, raised $5.5 million in five minutes. Augur, punting a proposition that decentralisation was a perfect mechanism to leverage the wisdom of crowds in the 'prediction' market (it was essentially an anonymous voting system to predict the future of, well, anything the Augur community deemed important), raised $5m in less than a day. A ICO for a company called Golem was nearly upended because there were too many buy requests in too short a time, clogging infrastructure along the way (in this case the servers taking the purchase requests). A browser project called Brave which used an underlying loyalty token called BAT hit its $35m target in 30 seconds.

It was not easy to distinguish which ICOs were legit. Or which were scams or well-intentioned but ultimately impractical ideas or 'money first–ideation later' chancers, or which were really never meant to be much more than a wink and a smile. JesusCoin for instance, which promised record transaction times between token holders and Jesus. Or the 'Useless Ethereum Token' which actually raised $75,000. Others soared to blinding market capitalisations and quickly collapsed, presumably making some of the founders rich in the process – FedoraCoin, PepeCash, the shamelessly named Einsteinium. And then there was TrumpCoin and PutinCoin, which also attracted some capital from who knows who. Celebrities didn't help. A number of them, clearly clueless as to what they were selling, shilled for new ICOs, adrenalised by the free tokens they had received in payment. And as we know, celebrity influencers can now move markets, as evidenced by Elon Musk and his tweets in support of Dogecoin in 2021.

The ICOs started in 2014, when a total of $24m was raised, and then rose to a high of over $6bn in 2018, which included the startling one-year, $4.1bn raise for a blockchain called EOS, founded by a blockchain veteran named Dan Larimer (veteran is relative in this industry – Larimer is still in his 30s). The project has not met expectations, but is still a considerable player and there are still believers.

It had started to look like the ICO party would never end, notwithstanding some high-profile stories of ruin that had infiltrated the popular press. And then the SEC came calling, starting in 2017.

It had presumably taken the SEC this long to react not so much because they are incompetent (they are not), but because they were being very cautious in building their case, and because, well, it is a governmental body moving at its best pace, which is slow.

One of the most famous early projects in this space was The DAO, which was launched via ICO on April 30th, 2016. The project creators' big idea was that The DAO was to be a 'Decentralised Autonomous Organisation' by the very nature of its architecture. It was simply an organisation, but with no head and a flat democracy. Their plan was to raise money through the ICO, and then to have its token holders decide where and how to spend it. A sort of decentralised VC fund. No CEO, no managers, just token holders voting on spend submissions. This was an intriguing idea, one that had been long discussed. Decentralised payment and value transfer was all very well, but what about decentralised governance? A big idea, even very big, if you consider its possible use in democratic governments.

Sadly, the second reason for The DAO's fame, or more accurately notoriety, was that it got hacked: over $50m-worth (from $150m raised at its ICO). It was an enormous blow to the entire community, and particularly Ethereum, on which The DAO was built. It resulted in no less of an extreme reaction by Ethereum than a 'hard fork', which was essentially a new version of Ethereum, which included a patch of their core code, and an effective return of funds to those who had lost out. This was not the way things were supposed to work. Blockchains were supposed to be immutable. But the hard fork decision was taken, criticism was levelled far and wide, and the world continued.

Presumably the hack had focused the SEC's attention, and on July 25th, 2017 they released their report on The DAO. The ICO had violated SEC laws. The DAO ICO was the same as selling securities to the public. (It did not help that co-founder Christoph Jentzsch described participating in The DAO ICO as being similar to 'buying shares in a company and getting … dividends' in a YouTube video before the ICO.)

But there was a surprise in store. Instead of the founders doing the perp walk of shame into jail, the SEC lightly slapped them on the wrists. A warning only.

ICOs continued, likely relieved by the light sentence. But things slowed down; everyone knew that the SEC would get nastier, the warning having been just a shot across the bows. And this proved to be correct. Sanctions since The DAO became harsher and harsher. ICOs quickly died. There are other vehicles that have replaced ICOs, like the STO (Security Token Offering), but they look very much like traditional IPOs (Initial Public Offerings) in form, if not in substance.

But the Eureka moment of Steven Nerayoff and the support of Pryor Cashman put Ethereum in the clear, reiterated recently by the SEC. The ETH token has utility in the network, so it could not be classified as a share certificate. It does not pass the Howey Test.

And so, Ethereum had a clean bill of health, and DeFi surged forward on its sturdy back.

CHAPTER 7

Bridging DeFi and TradFi - stablecoins

Anyone with even a glancing interest in this world has been startled (and perhaps bemused as an observer, or terrified as a token-holder) by the extreme swings of price among the many tokens traded, some of them household names like Bitcoin, others less well known. Even Bitcoin swings have been dizzying, and it is considered the conservative old man of cryptocurrencies.

The following became obvious quite quickly – the cryptosphere needed a non-volatile peg. It needed a coin to be tied to the real world of fiat (government-backed) currencies, not the fizz and pop of cryptocurrencies wildly oscillating under the jackboot of fear and greed and the whims of happenstance.

And what could be better than the dollar price?

A 'stablecoin', a cryptocurrency pegged to the dollar price, would produce a slew of benefits. Forgive us for the death-by-PowerPoint list – it seems the easiest way to separate and summarise.

■   It would allow traders to easily enter and exit positions in different cryptocurrencies at low fees, without having to ever go back to fiat currency – representing a simple-to-operate medium of exchange.

■ It would allow traders to entirely exit their other cryptocurrency positions and hold their capital in the cryptosphere while plotting their next move.

■ It could have tax advantages in those jurisdictions which only make fiat currency profits reportable. For example, in Portugal, there is no tax on crypto capital gains.

■ It would completely avoid cryptocurrency price risk for non-instantaneous or time-conditional transactions. An example would be the purchase of a house using Bitcoin (this has been done numerous times). The buyer might need to wait for real-world matters, like the transfer of documents from a local government authority. Not wishing to be at the mercy of Bitcoin price movement, the transactor can park his funds in a stablecoin until all documents are received, avoiding the risk of Bitcoin price movement.

■ It would provide for auditability of exchange between cryptocurrencies in a way that is more secure than without stablecoins.

Most importantly, it would create a predictable and safe trading environment between banks and the cryptocurrency world, the final financial border between real and virtual. Concerns about volatility would be off the table. And a common language between traditional finance and cryptocurrencies is fundamental to the growth of this new monetary system, which has to work in parallel to TradFi for the foreseeable future. Not even the most radical of crypto-zealots would imagine otherwise.

And here an interesting philosophical fork appeared. One choice was to create a cryptocurrency and peg it to $1 in value, always. At any given moment, anyone could wire dollars (or yen or euros) from their bank to an exchange, and buy exactly that amount of a dollar stablecoin.

Tether was the first to market with the stablecoin USDT in 2014, co-founded by Brock Pierce, Craig Sellars and Reeve Collins, and it remains a huge force in crypto, with in excess of $65bn in USDT circulating at the time of writing. Tether was originally built on top of Bitcoin but has since expanded to Ethereum and other blockchains.

The amount of USDT purchased and distributed is supposed to match the amount of dollars held in Tether's USD fiat treasury. One needs to consider how important this is. If dollar reserves do not match the number of Tethers then the claim of $1 value is unprovable.

There have been doubts about this, and a couple of audits and related controversy around the nature of their reserves. Mischief in this regard is certain to bring regulators bearing pitchforks, and could crash confidence in the entire crypto sector. These concerns have not been entirely put to rest at the time of writing. This sort of financial vehicle is called fiat-collateralised stablecoin and is pretty simple to understand and implement. Other fiat collateralised stablecoins include USDC, PAXOS and TrueUSD, but Tether, having launched in 2014, is still the largest in the space, albeit with declining market share.

Which brings us to Rune Christensen. Rune is a Dane in his early 30s who majored in biochemistry, and later international business. He had his own approach about how to get a stablecoin a seat at the global crypto table, having a different idea about what a stablecoin was, how it should operate and who should govern it. He called it the DAI. With this in mind he started MakerDAO (not to be confused with The DAO) in 2014, which is generally credited as being the first 'true' DeFi project, still running strongly today.

His secret sauce – DAI would be collateralised by cryptocurrencies, not by fiat money.

One of the problems with MakerDAO, at least in explaining it to non-crypto experts, is that it introduced or fine-tuned a number of innovations at the same time, integrating them; some patience is needed to put it all together.

MakerDAO allows a participant to deposit a cryptocurrency (initially it was only ETH, though more cryptocurrencies have been facilitated since) and to receive DAIs in return. This is a perpetual loan against the ETH deposited; there is no term. Each DAI is worth $1, to do with as you please. A depositor sends ETH into a Maker 'vault', and the loan is sent to their wallet in DAI. This the buyer can use to buy other currencies or to exchange for fiat currency to buy a car or a jacket or a child's education.

We stop here for a moment to consider how revolutionary this is. Just this very simple explanation (which we will deepen momentarily) has already taken MakerDAO beyond what a bank can do. It has allowed a depositor to *take a loan against their own deposit in a different currency.* Imagine depositing dollars in your bank and then asking for a yen loan against it. Not likely in TradFi.

But there were still a few wrinkles to smooth out.

For instance, if the price of ETH were to suddenly plummet, Maker would be left holding a lower value in ETH than they loaned out in DAI. A recipe for insolvency. (As real-world example, if I were to hand over a gold ring to a pawnshop for a temporary cash loan, one can imagine the effect on the shop owner if the price of gold were to collapse before the cash was returned.)

So Maker requires that you can *only* borrow from Maker up to 66% of what you deposited, to guard against a collapse in price of your original crypto deposit. Still a great deal, still transformative, new, unprecedented, but now less risky for Maker by this forced over-collateralisation. Why transformative? Consider – you deposit 100 ETH, and borrow the DAI value of 66 ETH. So you now have a bunch of DAI to do with what you will, while your original 100 ETH remains with Maker, still yours. You cannot do this easily or instantaneously at a TradFi bank.

But wait, there's more. Everyone furrow their brows, because this is the clever part.

There is an interest rate charged against the DAI loan (just like there is with the use of your credit card), called the 'stability fee'. The quantum of the interest rate either encourages or discourages DAI being taken out of the pool, or returned. And this is the mechanism whereby they keep the dollar–DAI exchange rate equal to $1. Too many DAIs and its price will decrease, and vice versa, so in order to keep the price stable the contract algorithm needs to balance supply and demand via adjusting the stability fee. The entire Maker monetary system thereby acts as its own 'Federal Reserve', pulling the levers of interest rates to stabilise its internal economy, all performed algorithmically.

A final matter. The policies of MakerDAO are not set by Rune Christensen. The 'DAO' part of the name ('decentralised autonomous organisation') made it clear that its future was to be determined by its token-holders (the governance token is called MKR, which was released in an ICO in 2018) and not by an executive committee or CEO or board of directors. Token-holders decide the direction of the company. This is important and uncharted territory. At the time of writing MakerDAO was in the process of taking over the entire operation of Maker from the Maker Foundation (where Rune held important sway).

So what did Maker bring to DeFi?

It was the first currency to provide a crypto-backed stablecoin, pegged to the value of the dollar, facilitating a common currency language with which to interact with banks. It was the first project to offer a cross-cryptocurrency loan using a stablecoin. It was the first successful implementation of the long-discussed decentralised autonomous organisation, whose future was guided by holders of MKR, its governance token, also tradable on the open market. And finally, it was the first algorithmic-driven stablecoin, using the mechanism of a stability fee or interest payment to stabilise the internal economy of the system.

It may seem, superficially, that the stablecoin is not an earth-shattering innovation. But the success of Tether, DAI and, increasingly, other stablecoins has garnered increasingly passionate interest from central banks and large commercial partners (inasmuch as that industry can be said to feel passion). A cryptocurrency that mimics a national currency, but which can clear and settle in minutes rather than days – this prospect makes central bankers salivate as they consider the effect of vastly increasing velocity of currency. And not only because it annihilates counterparty risk (the risk that one party fails to hold up their end of a transaction).

There is a startling statistic from spring 2021. Coinmarketcap. com estimated that the annual trading volumes of all stablecoins was $16tr. That sounds like a lot. And it is, because the annualised trading volume of all US business–business transactions was about $25tr (according to Mastercard), which is not that much more. This seems impossible, given that stablecoins did not exist a mere five years earlier. It looks like a mistake in a spreadsheet. The total number of stablecoins in the hands of regular wallet-holders on any given day in spring 2021 was somewhere around $25bn. How, one may ask, does a daily outstanding balance of $25bn translate to an annual volume of $16tr? The answer is velocity. Stablecoins clear and settle instantly, and so are never stuck in some internal TradFi wait-state. The stablecoins are always available for another transaction, for more commerce. A given stablecoin moves through the digital world of commerce over 100 times per year, an order of magnitude more often than a fiat dollar. That's what policy makers want. Economic activity. The prospect of stablecoins supercharging the economy is not lost on central banks. Which is why national governments are suddenly taking notice of cryptocurrencies, DeFi, and the potential bridges between them and the old financial world.

Monetary historian Niall Ferguson is a recent convert to digital currency. In a 2020 podcast episode for the popular Unchained series, he talked with author Michael Casey about the antiquated US payment system and its tortuous clearing times, calling it 'largely a relic of the 1970s', but more pointedly he warned that there is a financial war on the go between China and the US. It is increasingly being fought with financial technology weapons, and China is clearly ahead with its more modern payment system. Both are chasing 'programmable currency' (with China again far ahead), a proxy for a smart-contract-based digital currency, a national crypto stablecoin.

The advantage gained by the winner will be incalculable. And DeFi has led the way.

CHAPTER 8

Depositing and lending: reinventing the core - Compound

The previous chapter discussed Maker, which roped a number of innovations into a complex and hardened knot early on in the development of DeFi. It is best known for the invention of the crypto-backed stablecoin DAI, but its entry into the lending market (loaning DAI against a number of other deposited cryptocurrencies) also catalysed a flurry of innovation in two of the pillar services on which banking has rested for over a thousand years – deposits and loans (or lending and borrowing, depending on your perspective).

It is worth recapping how all of this works in TradFi. There are two sorts of loans we might be exposed to in TradFi. The first is a loan for a substantive amount, to pay for a car or house or a new factory. These are facilitated by traditional banks, which use other depositors' money (and its fractional multiples) to offer loans at an interest rate higher than they are paying the depositor. The loans are generally contracted for a fixed term. Then there are short-term loans, where the pool of funds to loan exists in what is called the 'money market'. All sorts of money sloshes around the global financial ocean which is not tied to any long-term obligations at any particular point in time. Depositors have the ability to join these markets, which offer lower interest than fixed-term deposits. They are liquid and fat, given the great pool of unencumbered funds consistently becoming available as capital journeys its way in and out of more permanent appointments.

One of the largest of the DeFi projects in this sector is Compound. It was started by Robert Leshner and Geoffrey Hayes. Leshner looks very much like someone's really sweet older brother, a tad nerdy in a pleasant way and quick to smile, someone looking to make friends. But the new ideas that have continually gushed out of Compound are also evidence of keen prescience and intellect.

Leshner seems a little like an outsider in this space of technology swashbucklers, propeller-heads and edgy libertarians. Firstly he is an Ivy leaguer (University of Pennsylvania), he has an economics degree, and his CV lists, among other things, that he has held the chair of the San Francisco Revenue Bond Oversight Committee. Clearly not one you would expect to be wielding a sharpened sword at the front of the DeFi army.

The founders of Compound started developing their idea when ICOs had clearly come into the rifle sights of the SEC. So they made a key decision, and that was to approach the traditional world of venture capital, including those who had signalled an appetite for DeFi. As always, Andreessen Horowitz was there (a famously forward-looking VC company with their eyes firmly on the horizon, and with a new $2bn crypto fund announced in June 2021, the largest ever) along with a number of other high-profile investment companies like Bain Capital Ventures. In 2018 Compound raised their first round of $8.2m, and $20m a year later when it became evident that they were taking off.

Leshner is famously eager to help anyone who can help mature the sector, even competitors. This includes appearing on multiple podcasts and YouTube videos, evangelising Compound and talking about the business in general. He made a surprising statement in a podcast called Epicentre from July 2019. One of the hosts asked him about his business model. We don't have one, he admitted. Technology, security, end-users and ecosystem partners first, then worry about how to make money.

So we imagine the pitch to the venture capitalists. 'How are you going to give us a return on investment?', they might have asked. Either Leshner et al. had a reply which no one bought but they went ahead anyway, or they had big balls and said 'We don't know', or (more likely) the VCs said: 'Never mind profit. Build an impregnable ecosystem on top of which partners can scale your user base.'

Before we explain how Compound works, we need to talk about the concept of a liquidity pool. This is (as it sounds) a big pot of money, cryptocurrencies in our case. It is called a liquidity pool because the money is immediately available for various activities, and the pool is never empty. Which leads to two obvious questions. How do you get money into the pool, and how do you keep the pool from emptying out?

Hold that thought.

Compound's product is very easy to explain, but as usual, the details are what give it wings. Compound sought to have depositors provide money to the pool, and to have others borrow money from that pool, in a way that ensured stability and controlled risk. The liquidity pool in Compound is the same concept as the 'money market' described earlier. A pool of unencumbered money, provided by investors looking to park it for a while, for a fair return.

Banks, of course, also seek to lend out depositors' money to borrowers, and to control risk by ensuring that lenders repay. Except that banks take a profit from the spread between deposit interest rates and lending interest rates, as we have seen.

But Compound does not. The spread between the rates, which would normally constitute profit, is reinvested in the Compound pool (or vault) as ballast for stability, as added weight for liquidity. No wonder that the business model, the road to profit, was a little hard to gauge.

The process of incentivising people with discretionary funds to deposit those funds into the liquidity pool is called *liquidity mining*, which we will hear a lot about in many projects. (This, confusingly, is unrelated to the 'mining' we talked about in relation to cryptocurrency creation on Bitcoin. *Liquidity mining*, to put it simply, means the mining of investors' pockets for ready capital.) One could, like a bank in TradFi, offer an attractive interest rate in order to attract liquidity. But of course, so could every potential competitor. So Compound had a new idea. They would indeed offer the providers of liquidity interest in return for their deposited funds. But in addition, the depositor would be rewarded for their participation by being given a new token in return for their deposit, called a cToken, representing the principal amount plus interest, *which itself could be traded*.

So if you contribute DAI to the pool, you receive cDAI. If you contribute ETH, you receive cETH. If you withdraw your deposit by returning the cToken, you will receive your original tokens plus interest accrued. Why is this different from a bank? Because you can *sell* your cToken to someone else. Also, for those who are willing to do the analysis, you can invest your cToken into another product to try to get even better returns. This DeFi liquidity deposit simply has no equivalent in TradFi banking, at least not for the common bank customer.

And, as added gravy, liquidity providers would also receive Compound's governance token, called COMP, in proportion to how much they deposited (remember Maker's MKR token? Same idea). This token allows holders to vote on the governance of Compound – as in, what their roadmap should be, what changes should be made to the protocol, etc.

In addition, the governance token COMP can also be openly traded on crypto markets. It has seen a fivefold rise since its launch in July 2020. This has, at times, resulted in bizarre situations where investors were borrowing funds from Compound, and paying interest, not to use the funds but merely to get the price appreciation of the COMP governance token they were awarded, perhaps to sell on another market. The price appreciation made the interest payments affordable, and more.

So to recap, why deposit your money in Compound's liquidity pool? You will receive interest via the cToken awarded to you, accumulated nearly continuously (somewhere between fifteen seconds and a few minutes, traffic congestion-dependent). You can trade the cToken itself on exchanges. You have the ability to withdraw your deposit on demand. You will have a say in governing Compound's strategy via a publicly tradable governance token called COMP. And you can sell your COMP on another external exchange.

Pause here, if only to imagine a facsimile of this product at a high street bank. Deposit your money into our account, it would advertise. We'll pay you interest every minute or so. And as a reward we will let you join our board of directors. And you can sell your board seat in the open market. Oh, and we'll give you loyalty points that will probably go up in price. Yeah, right.

These incentive come-ons were and are at the heart of Compound's liquidity mining efforts. And it has worked – the liquidity pool attracted deposits immediately, grows daily, and shows no signs of slowing down.

Which brings us to the other side of the balance sheet from the liquidity deposits – the loans made by Compound to borrowers. Compound is multi-currency, meaning that there is a list of cryptocurrency choices that can be made by borrowers and lenders. This multi-currency capability also set Compound apart, at least at first. Other lending/staking projects like major competitor Aave have also migrated to multi-currency capability.

Much like the Maker protocol, borrowers have to over-collateralise by providing 50% more than they need, thereby protecting Compound against sudden adverse movements in price. Also, you never have to repay the loan (unlike with a bank). There is no term, so, again, it is a perpetual loan. If the collateral loses its value to the point of danger (because of adverse cryptocurrency price movement), the loan will automatically be liquidated.

Finally, all participants in the Compound marketplace are considered 'partners' in their ecosystem, and so borrowers are rewarded with COMP governance tokens when they interact with Compound in any way.

Which again leads to an amusing message if this happened in a real-world bank: 'Do business with us and you can sit on our board of directors.'

The most critical part of the entire protocol is how interest rates are set and how often they change – what is offered to depositors and what is charged to borrowers. It is, as in TradFi, the difference between success and failure; it is the balance which is the most difficult to achieve, and in the case of the very fast-moving volatility of

DeFi, the most complex. Unlike most banks, which have the luxury of dealing with very few fiat currencies (and generally only one), there are many cryptocurrencies and each has a different volatility and a different public confidence profile.

Compound takes an algorithmic approach to what interest rates are offered to depositors, except for the collar (minimum) and cap (maximum). Most are between 2% and 30%. This is set by Compound, with the firm intent to turn this process over to the COMP community, as Compound becomes, like Maker, governed by its users.

So there is centralised pegging of minimum and maximum rates by Compound management, but the actual rates offered and charged between those pegs are based on the mathematical formula of supply and demand, its workings visible in the smart contract. Unlike banks, the algorithm adjusts continuously as each block in the blockchain is filled. By having the smart contract automatically adjust rates depending on supply and demand, Compound is able to keep reasonable predictability and stability in its liquidity pools.

While the interest rates may rise and fall to stimulate or reduce demand or supply, there is still the matter of the 'quality' of the cryptocurrencies in the vault. A particular cryptocurrency may be considered safe one day but may subsequently be damaged by external factors (like a hack), while another coin may be 'pumped' by over-optimistic expectations. Robert Leshner has indicated that a 'quality' rating can only strengthen the ecosystem, and has coyly suggested that this might be a great partner project on top of Compound, or perhaps a project that should be left to some COMP token-holder in the Compound DAO to submit.

A question has been raised about the whole governance project, the utopian DAO. Not only of Compound, but of similar projects.

Are token-holders the right people to be making complex decisions about the future of a protocol? These protocols are clearly not simple to understand. COMP tokens can be held by anyone, many of whom would not care to participate in governance. And for those who do, there is no way to tell whether they know enough to make an informed decision.

Never mind Compound. Or DeFi. This question goes to the heart of democracy. Who is best situated to add value in any given community? Who is really qualified to vote? Again Leshner smiles at this question, and answers simply – perhaps some in the DAO could submit a proposal for the community to vote for a 'crypto-economist' to represent them. Perhaps a crypto-economist for each type of currency.

Aha. A US-style representative democracy! Let the people vote for their leaders to represent their constituency. No end of experimentation will be seen here in the coming years.

Leshner has spoken about how he sees, or hopes to see, the future, given Compound's relinquishing of control to the COMP token-holders and his personal aspirations to step back from leadership. He imagines Compound moving to a sort of foundation protocol, with a smorgasbord of applications lying on top, all using Compound's core functionality. A grand partner ecosystem dreaming up and developing things that the original Compound founders, or even their COMP-holders, would never have come up with.

Perhaps. What is certain is that Compound and its competitors, all offering different flavours and colours of the basic Compound model, are forging something unique in the history of finance. These include Aave, which has recently overtaken Compound in market capitalisation, as well as dYdX, Kava, Dharma and others.

There is another player that competes partly with Compound, deserving mention if only for the esteem in which its founder is held. This is Curve, started by Russian Michael Egorov, having already had a stellar early career in physics. His original idea, since expanded, was to create an exchange for stablecoins only, of which there are a number (DAI, USDC, USDT, etc.). The algorithm that he invented to execute the trade is sometimes referred to by admirers as 'moon math', and it resulted in very low price slippage and spread between the two trading counterparties – it was lower than anyone else was able to achieve. Curve has added other tokens to its exchange pool, as well as staking and lending functionality, and more recently time-locked loans called veCRV. Curve is highly respected in this field as one of its most consistent innovators.

In any event, this new DeFi sector dealing with deposits and loans fairly sparkles with bold experiments and new thinking. Some of them are going to get it right and embed themselves deeply into financial service ground. Even at this early stage the products they offer are simply beyond TradFi's capability to respond in kind, its systems being too ossified to change and compete effectively.

As we wrote this chapter, Compound had $18bn in its crypto money market, and $7bn out on loan. This company is a mere few years old, competing directly with massive forces of traditional finance.

That is an astonishing success, by any measure.

A final new innovation needs mention. The world of DeFi lending – and specifically the collateral required to secure a loan – has been, until recently, in the closed world of cryptocurrency. The lender is required to deposit one type of cryptocurrency in order to loan another. TradFi collateral does not work this way. Long-established processes have enabled borrowers to lock up their homes or other assets (like equity or other business assets) as security. Defaults are not pretty, obviously, with homes repossessed by banks, and companies forced to liquidate. But it happens every day – loans secured by real stuff is standard banking business.

A number of new crypto companies are using blockchain technology to absorb physical assets into collateral instruments, using a type of Ethereum protocol called an NFT, which is simply a crypto-secured title deed, immutable and tamper-proof, and governed by a smart contract (which, of course, allows infinite flexibility in setting rules). New DeFi entrants like Centrifuge have already started to integrate with crypto lenders, opening up a potentially massive new portal between digital and real financial worlds. Indulge our brevity here – we will cover NFTs in greater detail later in these pages.

CHAPTER 9

Yield farming and Yearn

There was a period of DeFi history now fondly called 'The Summer of DeFi', which began around mid-2020 and lasted well into December. How it started is a little difficult to pin down, but observers have pointed to Compound, and in particular the launch of COMP as a governance token, and secondarily (or primarily, depending on your level of cynicism) an incentive to deposit funds in Compound's liquidity pool, more likely a little of both. Compound was not the first to offer incentives – that honour went to a project called Synthetix – but Compound had made a larger splash at the time; they are remembered as the spark.

This was the start of the liquidity mining wave. Incentives were dreamed up by multiple projects to attract capital which could then be deployed in support of whatever crypto service was being built and offered to the public. As described previously, Compound needed capital in its pool (or 'vault') in order to lend cryptocurrency out to borrowers, all of whom would have had their own reasons for the loans – ranging from a short-term need for real dollars to a desire to leverage up for another crypto investment.

More importantly, all of these projects that were mining liquidity, including Compound, had different schemes to attract capital.

It seems, from this remove, to have been a sort of bazaar, with barkers calling on passers-by to leave some capital at *their* stall, which would certainly, they would claim, give the best return. But there were enough projects for this to have been a head-scratcher. Where should I deposit my capital?, the confused return-seeking cryptocurrency-holder might ask.

In the world of TradFi, this is, at least in principle, a simple matter. If you can, deposit your money in the bank with the highest interest on offer. Of course, this is not simple in practice. Your current bank is not eager to see you go, and even if you do, the new bank is going to make you do onerous things like fill in application forms and show ID and wait for approvals.

To make matters worse, new crypto projects were appearing frequently, sometimes weekly, most of them aggressively seeking liquidity, mining our pockets furiously. They were designing ever more complex incentives, such as the cTokens and COMP that you met in the previous chapter. Projects with names like Balancer and Synthetix and Curve and Ren, as well as some of the newer decentralised exchanges (DEXs), have all devised clever incentives, sometimes fiendishly clever, and sometimes rather incomprehensibly clever.

This means that any crypto-holder, looking perhaps to get return for their passive assets like ETH or BTC, would be stuck having to do what is, sadly, an exhaustive amount of deep research to understand how the different projects reward investors.

And so to the arrival of 'yield farming', in which crypto-holders seek the best return from their money by constantly looking at the rates being offered by independent crypto projects and moving their tokens temporarily to the most attractive project before withdrawing and moving on to the next, or linking projects by lending from one to provide liquidity to another.

Would that it were so simple.

Enter Andre Cronje. Cronje was the brains behind Yearn, originally called iEarn. In January 2020 it was the first – and soon to become most famous – of the yield farming crypto projects, its original YFI token having a market capitalisation of over $1.2 billion at the time of writing (there are now other, newer tokens under the Yearn umbrella).

There are a number of things that set Cronje apart from most of DeFi. The first is that he is South African, a Cape Town resident, far away from the centres of crypto innovation, although it should be mentioned that a surprising number of other South Africans, especially from Cape Town, have found their way into the top rungs of crypto. And then there is the fact that Cronje did not award himself any tokens at all when they were first offered to the public. He originally funded the project from his pocket – his home mortgage, insurance, medical and other expenses having to be juggled like everyone else. He did not set himself up to get rich, unlike so many project founders who are now fabulously wealthy from their initial self-awarded token stashes.

Cronje tells us that it was not entirely altruistic. In the early days he was doing everything – design, coding, fixing, all the way down to technical grunt work. He now wanted the option to leave Yearn behind, to not be the source of all things Yearn, not to be the continual fountain of innovation. The best way to send this message was to own no governance tokens, which would pressure others to take on the work he had done alone.

Finally, Cronje, a former Computer Science educator, claims he is not a very good developer himself (a little far-fetched, I imagine, especially in the light of an impressive technology résumé), but it should not be forgotten that he built the prototype version of

Yearn alone. Completely alone. No team. Just him and his laptop. Cronje's Twitter bio used to say 'I test in prod'. Meaning that his test regime was running actual production software, live and in public – so use with caution. Those days are long gone now; Yearn is now hardened, it works.

The project has since attracted a large developer community and is no longer a one-man show. Cronje has often said he might move on to do something else. When he stops having fun, he will just hand over the metaphorical and spiritual keys. We suspect it is with some relief to the Yearn community that he has not done so yet.

Cronje's development of Yearn came from a personal desire to find who was offering the highest returns for the stablecoins he had in his wallet. He was, for lack of a better metaphor, simply looking for the best bank to put his money in. To do that he needed to look at each DeFi project live on Ethereum, and more specifically each smart contract, in order to understand how interest rates were calculated and what nuances and exceptions and wrinkles may have been embedded in the code. And with the arrival of the additional liquidity mining incentives in various projects – governance tokens and other specialty tokens – he dove deep, unravelling the economic interactions between all of the complex bits and pieces, and where the yield value might lie in myriad market circumstances.

What emerged from this effort was Yearn. The first version was straightforward: the Yearn smart contract sifts through multiple other projects, looking for the best return, and lodging capital there for as long as is necessary before withdrawing and lodging it elsewhere. It was a huge success, at least for Cronje's personal funds. The next step was to open this contract up to anyone who wanted to have access to the same yield farming tools. This would have an immediate benefit – as each new person interacted with the smart contract, so it would start another 'hunt' for the best deal, moving everyone else's coins there (called 'crop rotation', fitting in nicely with the farming metaphor). The more often this happened, the more continuously the yield was optimised for everyone, and the lower the aggregate transaction fees. The pool of money that was created as new people joined the 'world's smartest savings account' (as Cronje once called it) was named the yPool, and anyone who committed capital to the yPool was awarded with (you guessed it) the governance token YFI.

Cronje was very public about this token being valueless or at least having no 'price floor', a hypothetical 'cheap' price at which investors jump in. He says that he wanted to remove the investor mindset from the governance token, having become disillusioned by other governance tokens being used as speculation tools, which was never supposed to be their purpose, at least not officially. But because Yearn's governance token YFI was a publicly-traded token, his pleas went unheeded and the traders drove the price up 35,000% at one point.

How much does the yPool return to those who entrust their capital to it? Traditionally somewhere around 10% annual percentage yield. This number is variable and depends, obviously, on market conditions and the mix of crypto tokens that are being considered. But consider that most banks, at least in the US and Europe, are offering 1% return and less. 10% is eye-poppingly attractive.

Cronje has since released a number of new products under the Yearn umbrella, including newer pools designed partly in collaboration with DeFi projects where capital is to be committed, although in a recent podcast he ruminated on the original version of Yearn, V1 as he named it, his first baby, which he designed in collaboration with Michael Egorov of lending platform Curve. He indicated it was still his favourite. Simple, immutable, impervious to external influences, unsullied by too much complexity. Easy to implement (at least relative to later Yearn products) and more importantly, easy to explain. It bears repeating. Yearn would do all the heavy lifting for investors, finding the best return from all liquidity providers, putting investor funds into the best current liquidity pool. It also straightforwardly returns whatever token was used to participate, and protects against losses. The worst-case scenario from using V1 is that you will get your original token balance back. That is a very simple and compelling value proposition.

What Cronje did with Yearn V1, and subsequent versions, raises an important concern. It is that finance is complex. Risk is complex. Trade is complex. Whether it be in DeFi or in TradFi, there are layers of functionality in any financial system that are a direct consequence of the human condition. Whom to trust. How to adjudicate value. The entire edifice of society is built on complex social intercourse; and the exchange of value between humans is among the most complex, because it usually pits one person's opinion against another's. How much is it worth, the thing we are exchanging? And how do incentives alter the perception of worth?

Entire civilisations hinge on these questions. Whether it be food, or shelter, or gold, or skills, or the dollar – or even someone's life – the question of worth, price, and value resonates through our societal systems, and is quantified and codified and made executable and transactable through economic, financial, legal and political systems.

So it is no surprise that thousands of years of civilisation have moulded systems of great complexity to answer these questions, all the way up from the personal level to governments that set and calculate the value of the machinery of monetary exchange.

DeFi is a rewiring of these mechanics, using a new set of tools. But like the old system, and some of the parts DeFi will eventually replace, it is not simple. Not in the design of its smart contracts and not in the interaction of its 'money legos' – the name given to well-defined financial smart contracts that are available to everyone to plug in to their applications. These allow the building of even bigger and more complex financial instruments by having smart contracts interact with and use other smart contracts. The underlying complexity of DeFi smart contracts, the depth of the architecture of blockchain, and the infinite 'composability' of money legos act as an Achilles heel to fast public adoption.

And so these new tools of finance are not easy to explain, which brings us back to Yearn. Cronje built his original system to find the best return for his own crypto savings. He did the hard work of understanding the complexity of the various deals on offer, and built a system to find the best one, and then offered it to anyone who wanted it, shielding them from the detailed analysis that none of us have time for.

And then it got a little more interesting. His next version, V2, went a step further, in that it allowed *redeployment* of the incentives offered by the various projects back into high-paying DeFi vehicles, which bumped up annual percentage yields to around 15% at the time of writing (depending, again, on the weather).

At this point submissions started to pour in from the Yearn community, COMP token-holders making suggestions for even smarter strategies for even larger yields. These were much more complex than those on offer – take this coin and invest it in that pool and move 50% of this incentive to this leveraged instrument before hedging against that derivative, etc. The Yearn team were now faced with a new problem: how to test and manage and release all the new ideas, many of them labyrinthine builds of convoluted 'lego money models'.

So V3 was released, which allowed any community participants to design a yield farming strategy of arbitrary complexity, lock it up in a 'vault' and allow anyone to use it. It would, like much else in this new world, be Darwinian. If the strategy produced superior return, it would survive and thrive. If it started to fail, investors would move elsewhere.

We pause again here to consider TradFi. There is simply no reasonable facsimile for this. There are, to be sure, financial advisers who will advise on which savings deposit or government debt instrument or stock or bond in which to invest. Fancier 'robo advisers' will now even do this without human intervention. But in Yearn V3, you have developers and financial engineers building new products all the time and delivering them to a vault to be tested and exploited by anyone who cares to do so, whose real-time yield returns are a matter of public record, and the internal logic of which is open for anyone to inspect. What usually takes many years of deliberation in the TradFi world – product development – is now reduced to hours or even minutes in DeFi, with rapid testing.

Cronje has expressed some discomfort with Yearn V3, at least in comparison to his original V1. The strategies invented and coded by community contributors in the V3 vaults are like living organisms, hard to manage and predict, extremely difficult to analyse. There is clearly a loss of control as these yield crops sprout and bloom. Many will wither; this is not a problem. But others may do damage, a greater risk for Yearn.

The nature of DeFi and smart contracts and money legos has unleashed an army of farmers (the word is too pallid – 'hunters' would be more accurate), all of them deploying new technologies as weapons as they seek the best deals. Similar armies have been deployed before, in the days of the early Internet, where lone programmers wrote programs to trade on public markets, seeking patterns and arbitrage and edge. Many of them were eventually subsumed into fast-moving companies with blazing fibre connections to exchanges and clever algorithms, such as those famously described by Michael Lewis in his book *Flash Boys*. And then into heated brain trusts with clumps of PhDs at massive investment companies like Goldman Sachs. But as markets seek price efficiency (as they always tend to do), so these TradFi wizards find it harder and harder to achieve their edge.

With DeFi still a newborn baby, and yield farming newer still, we predict that sensational returns will be found for a while yet, as new projects with fancy incentives continue to come online. There will be stories of wealth made and perhaps ruination too. And as one protocol presents unprecedented yields, so will new challengers rise up to beat it, along with hunters that flock to the pools offering the highest returns, which are then eventually diminished as they are hunted to extinction.

And then, we predict, some time in the future, yields will, must, revert to a more modest mean, just as traditional money markets have settled on predictable, stable, and comparatively modest returns. It is a mathematical certainty.

Cronje and the people at Yearn, meanwhile, have been branching into all manner of new DeFi projects, including insurance. It seems that there will be much more to talk about at Yearn, even after pure yield farming has become a little staid.

CHAPTER 10

Decentralised exchanges (DEXs) and Uniswap

In researching the history of exchanges, it is striking how much of the literature is about stock exchanges, at least those that rise to the top of the search engines. But, of course, exchange in its purest form has been around for as long as humans have, via barter. One source claims that barter was invented by Mesopotamian tribes in 6000 BCE, and improved by Phoenicians and Babylonians as goods were transported and exchanged across ever-increasing distances. It is a little hard to believe this claim, or at least to pin a date for the 'invention' of bartering. It seems to be such a basic instinct; it is in fact central to all sorts of cultural mythologies.

But there were developments which increased the reliability and efficacy of exchange, and the first of those were the tools of weights and measures, which allowed a crude sort of value to be assigned – the weight of a bag of salt or the number of glass beads, for example. And then, at least partly in historical parallel, the development of tokens of exchange, from cowrie shells and baboon bones to gold coins, which changed trade matters irrevocably. Money – or IOU notes between people – is about as old as language.

History shows societies and communities dripping with markets and souks and bazaars, where tokens of value were (and still are) used as a proxy for barter. But urbanisation quickly led to situations where there were simply too many people jockeying for trade, where supply and demand was hobbled by the logistics of attending to buyers and sellers at scale, with speed, accuracy and fairness.

Which of course led to the formal exchange, wherein a trusted central authority was tasked with organising the 'order book' – listing who had intent to buy, who had stuff to sell, what was offered and what was bid. The trusted authority took care of the books, finding and matching buyers and sellers whose price requirements were close enough to make a deal and calculating and displaying prices of assets, and later, other metrics like volume of traded value.

Which is where it has been for hundreds of years, with all the innovations clustered around matters of speed, price discovery, accuracy, data analytics, settlement and auditability, and regulation. Exchanges, particularly the great stock exchanges we are all familiar with, are massively liquid, with electronic orders matched and concluded in fractions of seconds (for a fee), and all manner of fancy order types supported, further democratised beyond the financial elite by the offering of services in well-designed and easy-to-use PC and mobile trading apps.

But it's all still centralised, with exchanges acting on behalf of buyers and sellers, and extracting a fee for services. For DeFi engineers and developers of smart contracts in the DeFi community, this was an appetising opportunity for disruption.

There were, even prior to the arrival of DeFi, a number of crypto exchanges. The largest players in this field are the centralised exchanges, now a multibillion-dollar industry, with names like Kraken and Huobi Global and Binance and Coinbase (whose valuation peaked at a startling $96bn on the day of its public listing in 2021, focusing the world's financial attention on the previously nerdy world of crypto exchanges). But these are all massively centralised. They take control of your funds; they manage private keys on your behalf – those digital keys which give access to your funds.

Unsurprisingly, a few of these centralised exchanges have been hacked for enormous amounts, had technical snafus, suffered from downtime, had poor customer service, and unilaterally changed policies. Some have even been outright scams, like Canada's QuadrigaCX with its fake order books and the intriguing story of a CEO who 'died' while holidaying in India after emptying out exchange wallets.

All of which makes decentralisation proponents very tetchy. What was needed were decentralised exchanges (DEXs) that allowed traders to exchange currencies and other crypto-assets with each other without anyone in the middle, cocooned by the same protections and advantages of permissionless, secure, trustless decentralised services.

There had been a number of these attempts even prior to Ethereum in 2015, starting with NXT and Counterparty on Bitcoin. But the Bitcoin blockchain was difficult to wrangle for new services other than for its original purpose, so after the launch of Ethereum and its Solidity-based smart contract platform, a new crop of DEX aspirants arrived on the stage, with names like IDEX and EtherDelta and others. All had good ideas, all suffered from flaws of one kind or another – like limited asset tradability, or only partial decentralisation. There were also issues of scalability, user experience, absence of analytics, and more. But those were engineering problems, easily solvable.

The biggest barrier of all was liquidity.

Sarah Austin, head of content for DeFi company Kava Labs, expressed this concisely in a recent article: 'Without a decent number of users, prices were easy to manipulate and liquidity was impossible to maintain. This produced a Catch-22 situation: users won't come if there isn't enough liquidity, but without users, there is no liquidity. Users remained trading on Centralised Exchanges where companies and large traders were more confident of higher volumes due to better availability of supply.'

Enter Hayden Adams, a 26-year-old mechanical engineer just laid off from Siemens in 2017, anxious about his future. He called a college friend, Karl Floersch, who was working at the Ethereum Foundation and had been sucked into crypto immediately after college, while Hayden had chosen a more traditional engineer's path. Here, according to Hayden, is how the conversation unfolded:

Hayden: I just got laid off :(
Karl: Congratulations, this is the best thing that could
    have happened to you!!! Mechanical Engineering is a
    dying field. Ethereum is the future and you're still early.
    Your new destiny is to write smart contracts!
Hayden: Don't I need to like know how to code?
Karl: Not really, coding is easy. Nobody understands how
    to write smart contracts yet anyway.

What Hayden did was build a decentralised crypto exchange called Uniswap within a year or so, as we will see shortly, but take a moment to consider this – he didn't know how to code. This entire field was so new, so unmoored to tradition and so fluid, that young people with almost any background could pile in and build something great.

Hayden, who looks like an extra from the TV show *Silicon Valley*, was still living with his parents, and started to teach himself blockchain basics and Ethereum and its programming language Solidity, as well as the language Javascript (a *lingua franca* of basic programming taught to undergraduates the world over). He was hooked immediately.

This story, like many great stories, needed a catalysing event. That was provided by Vitalik Buterin.

Around the time of Hayden's entry into this world (he was still a neophyte, and didn't know anyone in the industry besides Karl) Buterin had posted a blog and a Reddit post. Both pieces of content are fairly dense, but well within the grasp of anyone with junior college maths and a little determination (only high school maths, really). But rather than crawl through Vitalik's problem description and suggested path to solution, it is probably more instructive to talk about the concept of a 'market maker' in the TradFi world of exchanges.

The major constraint of a centralised exchange is that an order book needs to be maintained, buyer–seller pairs need to be found at a single point in time, and need to mutually agree on price, so that the trade can be concluded. The system needs to continually line up buyers and their bids, sellers and their offers, and try to get them to make a deal. Often, in illiquid markets, buyers and sellers are too far apart, and deals are not made. Or buyers and sellers are not looking to trade at the same time. Both of these slow down trade velocity, reducing exchange profits and leaving buyers and sellers unsatisfied (and their aspirations thwarted).

So, the 'market maker'. This was a concept pioneered by exchanges to ensure speed and liquidity in a well-functioning market. In order to simplify this concept, imagine a really rich person who has enough capital to *always* and *immediately* buy *or* sell an exchange product, like a stock. They (the market maker) advertise a buy price and a sell price, which continually change. Our rich person is a keen observer of supply and demand, and they know when and how to adjust prices to attract buyers and sellers. And to compensate for the risk of getting in trouble (perhaps because the market suddenly shifts), the market maker takes the spread between the advertised buy price and sell price, and pockets it. It is the risk premium they award themselves. And in many exchanges, there are competing market makers – the ones best able to foresee the risk, to reduce the spread, and to offer the best prices for buyers and sellers will get richer faster (a note of cynicism here – it seems to us that all market makers get rich, because they are generally large institutional insiders and the rest of us are mere traders).

So, to repeat. The market makers are always there to take a trade, so the furious and hopeful matching of individual buyers and sellers (even when done via computers) is not a requirement. Market makers are like a beloved but kleptomaniac uncle, always there when you need him, even if he rifles a few pennies from your jacket pocket.

The concept of market maker is simple, but it got a little more complicated when applied to crypto. There are no rich uncles in crypto, only smart contracts. How did someone like Hayden Adams imagine he was going to attract a pool of capital to fund the 'Automated Market Maker' pool of capital? And even if he did, traditional market makers were exchanging money for stocks. In this new world there was a need for multiple different tokens being cross-exchanged with each other, a level of complexity higher than merely cash for stocks. And further, cryptocurrencies were then, and still are, subject to wild and often unpredictable swings in volatility, making the automated market maker calculations of buy and sell prices much more fraught.

Buterin's two posts articulated the pricing problem and suggested some approaches (leaning on the work of a number of others in the field). It is instructive to read the blog post (the link can be found at the end of this chapter), not so much to understand the maths, but to get a feel for the exacting nature of his inquiry, and his articulation of the issues. What he was saying was – here's a cool project. Also an important project. Here are some ideas. Anyone interested in this?

At this point Hayden had learned enough about Ethereum and coding to start looking for a real project to chew on. The two serendipitous Buterin posts had suddenly given him his handrails, and so he started his climb. By this point he had started to meet people, introduced first by his friend Karl Floersch, then by his increasing attendance at various crypto workshops, drop-ins and conferences.

We are going to skip over the mathematics of the token pricing and token balancing and the related price spread scenarios, but the principle is simple.

There is a direct relationship between the number of tokens in the pool and the total dollar value of the pool – simple arithmetic. As traders buy and sell tokens, the total number of coins in the pool changes as some tokens flow in and others flow out. The price of these tokens must change if the pool is to have a constant value (which it must – this is the key principle enforced by the algorithm, called the 'Constant Function Market Maker').

OK – so now you have a situation where token prices are sliding up and down as tokens move in and out of the pool. Which opens the door to the art of arbitrage, in which traders throughout history have sought to spot a temporary difference between the price of the same asset traded on two different markets, and to take advantage of it by buying at the lower price and selling at the higher price. Which means that there is an opportunity for traders to arbitrage between another market (like Coinbase) and Hayden Adams' Uniswap pool as a token price in the pool gaps away from average prices on other global crypto markets. Which ... quickly brings the prices back into line with global prices. It is a self-regulating system. That's why arbitrage always has a limited lifespan. By its very nature a price gap is exploited until the gap is closed.

So traders looking for a quick profit from slightly different pricing on other markets serve to keep Uniswap prices from drifting too far away from average prices. Very, very clever. For those interested in the underlying maths (which is pretty straightforward), we will post a link to one of the many YouTube videos on the subject at the end of the chapter.

Eureka. A simple method of pricing tokens and balancing the economics of the pool, in real time and with little risk, even in fast-moving markets, simply by attracting external profiteers to stabilise price. It is the economic supply and demand pricing model writ large. We are skipping over multiple complexities here, of course. But the important take-away is that an algorithmic token market making model could be implemented.

And now we move onto the next problem, the market maker described earlier in the chapter, that pool of funds that allows instant fulfilling of orders. How to attract liquidity to the market maker pool, or AMM (automated market maker) as it is now commonly called in the world of smart contracts? This was a much simpler problem, because it had been done many times before in other projects. But instead of offering liquidity providers the incentive of high interest rates and/or free governance tokens (as in Compound and others), Uniswap liquidity providers would be offered a cut of the trade, specifically a cut of the spread between the buy and sell price. All liquidity providers became, in effect, crypto-brokers, their income growing as more and more traders used Uniswap to trade. And again, in keeping with the extraordinary democratising architecture of trustlessness, permissionlessness and decentralisation, everyone and anyone could participate, without regard to wealth or bloodline or connections in the industry or IDs or any other barriers to entry. Traders saw fast, accurate, inexpensive and fairly executed trades, and liquidity providers got a fair return for their capital. And as has become de rigueur for projects in DeFi, UNI is Uniswap's governance token, distributed free to early users of the system and thereafter, and itself traded on public exchanges.

We pause here to talk about IDs (identification documents). These are mandatory to gain access to traditional exchanges, for a number of reasons including crime prevention, tax collection and investor protection. DEXs are fiercely resisting this, wishing to give traders totally unsupervised access to do what they wish with their money. And given that DEXs are decentralised and dispersed among thousands of participants, there is no owner, company or entity to hold responsible. Moreover, these sort of user verifications are very difficult to implement – the smart contracts which govern DEXs cannot be changed and nor can they be written to facilitate KYC (Know Your Customer). This matter sits at the heart of the decentralisation debate, and tempers easily flare around what is a complex set of principles that define the line between individual and state.

Uniswap V1 launched with immediate success on Ethereum on November 12th, 2018. Since then V2 and V3 have been released, each with increasingly important new trading functionality. While the substance of some of the new functionality is beyond our scope, we repeat what has become a mantra in this book. TradFi exchanges cannot compete with the AMM-based exchanges. The DeFi DEXs are moving too fast, and adding features in a matter of months that would take a major exchange years, even decades to implement.

This has led to a fascinating new development, and that is the tokenisation of traditional assets – gold, stocks, bonds and their ilk, a potentially massive new market of DEX-traded crypto derivatives of real-word items, which we will cover in detail later in the book. But what seems clear to us is that all TradFi and centralised crypto exchanges will be forced to migrate to DEX-style technologies; it will soon be an existential risk they cannot avoid.

There are numerous side-alleys to this story. The first is that although Uniswap is the largest DEX by volume (over $1bn per day at the time of writing) there is fearsome competition, some of which predates Uniswap. Curve, Balancer, dYdX, Bancor, 1inch, SushiSwap, PancakeSwap, CowSwap, 0x and others, all competing furiously to add the fanciest new features and financial algorithms, sometimes darting ahead in the race for 'look-at-what-I've-got' for a short time, while competitors regroup to think up something smarter. And some are migrating off Ethereum as the network becomes ever more congested and expensive and onto other new blockchain initiatives like Solana, BSC, PolkaDot, Cosmos and others.

SushiSwap (part of a weird cult-like obsession with food names within the industry, including the term 'foodcoin') has its own story. As part of the uncompromising libertarian leanings of the crypto community, almost everything is open-source, free for inspection, critique and improvement suggestions. SushiSwap was an unapologetic copy of Uniswap, its name changed, and then a few new features added. There have been, and still are, concerns, discomfort and a little rage over the ease with which SushiSwap copied hard-worked innovations and reshaped them into competition. But we suppose that is the price of openness, and it has happened many times in this wide-open industry.

Although there was at least one strange consequence to this, the matter of SushiSwap's incentive program, which was aggressively marketed to Uniswap liquidity providers who quickly migrated to SushiSwap, receiving generous swag bags of Sushi governance tokens. Sushi's value increased quickly as demand rose on markets and caused a 'vampiric draining' of Uniswap, with liquidity providers migrating to SushiSwap simply to take advantage of fast-rising incentive token prices. The details of this are strange but true – traders and speculators twisting momentarily inefficient markets to their needs. A staggering $1bn was drained from Uniswap pools in days, giving SushiSwap the liquidity springboard it needed to start trading. This sort of thing happens frequently in these wild times. In some interpretations it is the lawless, unregulated and sometimes ethically questionable behaviour of profit-seekers. In others, it is the rules of the game, and it drives innovation.

Either way, it is unlikely to end any time soon.

Vitalik Buterin posts:
https://vitalik.ca/general/2017/06/22/marketmakers.html
https://www.reddit.com/r/ethereum/comments/55m04x/
lets_run_onchain_decentralized_exchanges_the_way/

Constant Function Market Maker algorithm explained:
https://www.youtube.com/watch?v=Ui1TBPdnEJU

CHAPTER 11

Oracles!

'... a quadrillion dollars in value ...'

I t was too much of a temptation to pass up this piece of a quote from Sergey Nazarov (CEO of Chainlink), whom we will meet later, mainly because of his casual use of 'quadrillion'. It wasn't hyperbole. It is a real number, the estimate of the global value of derivatives – options, futures, swaps, forex (foreign exchange) spreads, etc. It is one thousand trillion dollars, ten times the world's GDP. There is some minor quibbling about this number, because it is apparently hard to measure, but no matter; its scale has direct bearing on what is to follow, so sorry for the teaser, but read on.

One of the great beauties of blockchain technology is its stern and unshakeable determinism. It has existed in a walled garden, where everything is cryptographically provable, tamper-proof and locked in for all time. Where transactions initiated outside the chain and sent to it are securely processed and recorded and frozen in time.

We, however, exist in a very different natural world. Non-determinism abounds. Unpredictable events happen. It is unreliable. It is in many important ways *untrustworthy*. We cannot see (or at least cannot see clearly) the future. To put it plainly, shit happens.

Because we are concerned with decentralised finance, we give you a simple example. What is the price of Bitcoin right now? Or the $/EU exchange rate? You could go and look it up of course, but how much do you trust the data source? How do you know they are giving you the true numbers? Worse, how do you know that some malware in your laptop or smartphone didn't change the number before it reached your screen?

Here's another: you may check the price of gold now and assume it will be about the same tomorrow, without finding out that someone overnight in China has found a cheap way to chemically reproduce it and said so on Twitter. Or maybe you couldn't predict the effects on the price of orange juice futures of an unseasonal overnight freeze in Florida.

'Blockchains are blind to the real world,' says Giulio Caldarelli of the University of Verona. They were not built to worry about orange juice. Which leads to a statement of the 'problem'. How does one open a sightline from the deterministic world of blockchains to the non-deterministic world of real life?

Why, one may ask, do we even need to? None of this was particularly important in the early days. The Bitcoin blockchain was designed to wrangle Bitcoins from one address (or 'wallet') to another – to transact and settle with certainty; no one cared about the price of a house or the price of gold or the weather report. With the arrival of Ethereum and the smart contract, a few people started to lift their heads from their code and to see the world around them, but so many of the original explorers were digging away at DEXs and yields and stablecoins and lending; the real world could wait.

But these were the early days of DeFi; the ongoing reinvention of finance. Traditional finance had other inputs – prices, value, rates, ratios, balance sheets, revenues, tonnage, volumes. Real things in the real world. DeFi would never have an impact on much unless there was interbreeding of these two species – real and virtual.

Which led slowly, and then quickly, to the notion of oracles. For anyone remembering their Greek mythology, oracles were sources of infinite wisdom and knowledge due to their special relationships with the gods of Mount Olympus. They provided information and knowledge to travellers and other seekers. They were guardians of truth.

Sergey Nazarov has been around crypto since the very early days of Bitcoin. Like many others who were present at the birth of the industry, it has been argued that he is Satoshi Nakamoto, which he denies, as does every other person similarly accused (people being fingered as Satoshi has become something of a spectator sport, but an increasingly irrelevant one).

Nazarov had arrived in New York with his Russian parents, both engineers, in the 1990s. He was, like so many who have found their home in crypto, a videogame obsessive. Also a Lego-obsessive. A rip-the-TV-apart-and-see-how-it-works obsessive. A devourer of programming manuals. And, after a non-technical degree and some teaching, discovering Bitcoin in the early 2010s and falling in love and becoming, well, a crypto-obsessive.

He started a company called SmartContract in 2014, but it was not until much later in 2017 when Chainlink launched.

Chainlink, unlike all the other projects described so far, is not a blockchain protocol, nor is it a smart contract. Its mission is entirely different, and that is to supply real-world data to smart contracts in a way which is, to the greatest extent possible, trustworthy. This is a tall order. The demand for these external data services began to grow quickly in 2017. As smart contracts emerged from the sea and crawled onto dry land, so did the need to interact with real-world data.

This presented a dilemma. Blockchains are, to all intents and purposes, perfectly trustworthy. The whole crypto ecosystem is. So if this ecosystem is to interact with external data, then how does one make that system trustworthy enough? How high or low is the bar? What does it mean to be 'trustworthy enough' for consideration by smart contracts where there may be much at stake?

Nazarov evolved a solution that approached the problem from a number of perspectives. Firstly, his architecture mandated the creation of a number of 'nodes' or 'oracles', collectively known as an oracle network. This network itself was decentralised, with no single point of failure. Each node would then connect to one or more external data services, which would be used by smart contracts requiring some external data to process transactions.

Let's say a smart contract requires the Apple stock price from the external world. The developers of this smart contract believe that if five oracles agree on a price, then it is trustworthy. The oracles on the network retrieve the price – one from Bloomberg, one from the Nasdaq exchange, one from Yahoo Finance, etc. If all oracles agree on the price, it then becomes accessible to the smart contract (multiple upstream data providers are not always possible, and sometimes there is only one provider of data, like a government agency).

There is an important principle in this example. The developers of this hypothetical contract were happy with a five-oracle consensus; the smart contract enforces the sanctioned number of agreeing oracles they would deem to be trustworthy, not Chainlink. Which brings us to our opening quote about 'a quadrillion dollars'. The level of trust is in direct proportion to the size of the risk. Smart contracts which are dealing with large amounts of money will demand greater decentralisation of the oracle network, with more nodes achieving consensus.

The real-world derivatives that comprise that quadrillion dollars are swarming to DeFi, which is a perfect vehicle to execute the business of computing the sometimes arcane mathematics of these complex financial instruments. Billions in crypto derivatives are already sloshing around the Ethereum blockchain on projects like Synthetix. Maybe not quadrillions yet, but growing fast. And with numbers like those, you had better trust your data.

The second item in Nazarov's architecture was to protect the data from manipulation somewhere between the oracle network and the blockchain (called the man-in-the-middle attack). This is achieved via the methodology of public key cryptography described earlier.

Chainlink has also attended to developer tooling to make data providers' lives easy. The company has provided technology kits to allow the oracle nodes themselves to develop and lodge 'data smart' contracts directly on the Ethereum blockchain. A smart contract for this data, a smart contract for that data, etc. This was an important development – DeFi app developers who seek to interact with data (such as those who need prices from an external market) just interact with the appropriate 'data' smart contract – which is just another 'lego' piece on the blockchain, available for use.

Clearly, Chainlink wanted as many nodes or oracles as possible to participate in the oracle network – with each additional node meaning greater tamper-resistance. This was achieved using the same incentives as many other projects we have discussed. Node participants are awarded LNK tokens – governance tokens, tradable on markets. At the time of writing there were over 130 nodes, representing over 600 feeds from over 100 data sources. Given the amount of data flowing about the planet, we expect that this number will grow rapidly, especially as smart contracts grow more specialised (like sports betting) and, in some cases, more localised (like the price of grapes in France).

Building a system to enable smart contracts to access external data had an inverse benefit. Smart contracts could use the same ecosystem to send data back to the outside world – for instance, payment advice to a traditional payment provider like Stripe. Very useful indeed, expanding the horizons for smart contracts immeasurably. For example, imagine a smart contract that ingests an external interest rate and then, if other conditions are satisfied, instructs the bank to make a real-world payment. External data in (interest rate), external data out (payment instructions).

There are other matters around the Chainlink story which are of interest. Nazarov realised that having a 'middleware' layer of decentralised off-chain nodes to mediate between external world data and smart contracts would also open opportunities for those nodes to do other things that are impractical or difficult on the blockchain, beyond just the transmission of external data.

Remember that smart contracts were intended to carry out fairly specific tasks – they were never designed to be general-purpose computer programs such as may be found in the real world. It became possible to imagine use-cases where the smart contract would have its needs best serviced off-chain, for reasons of speed, perhaps, or the power of a general-purpose programming language to carry out some intensive and scary compute problem. This was simple to achieve, but in order to offer the smart contracts a level of trustworthiness that they expected (moving stuff out of the contract and off the chain gives smart contract developers nightmares), Nazarov mandated that a hardware-based secure compute environment exist at the nodes, in those cases that needed it. He settled on a technology developed by Intel, in which an 'enclave' is instantiated in the secure hardware, allowing non-tamperable and private compute operations outside of the prying eyes of anyone, including the node operators. There are some players whose scepticism around this is on loud display – once it is out of the smart contract and off the blockchain, disaster awaits, they warn. Perhaps, but the fact that the 'secure enclave' code is being executed by many nodes in the decentralised network at the same time produces, for some contract developers, an acceptable risk profile.

Chainlink has also instituted a 'reputation rating' for nodes. Nodes that deliver poor data or are not responsive in some other way are given a dreaded demerit, and can eventually be forced from the oracle network. And because nodes are incentivised by LNK rewards, quality of performance gets baked into the relationship between Chainlink, its nodes and its smart contract developers.

Which brings us to some of the interesting things being done using Chainlink and nodes and external data. The Internet of Things (IoT), for instance – hardware sensors in the real world. Environmental data is streamed into the node, validated, and sent to a contract which has need of such information, such as temperature or moisture for an agricultural insurance DeFi application.

Chainlink also provides random numbers to any contract that requires them. Random numbers? Yes. Endlessly useful in myriad applications. There is no random number generator native to the smart contract. If you want one, go ask the oracles. How about GPS data? Who needs this? Well, imagine a smart contract that pays out only when a ship docks.

Chainlink and others have changed the game, in giving smart contracts a much larger toolbox with which to build things. Competitors include BAND, DIA, Tellor, and API3. There is no shortage of innovation in this portal that connects blockchains to the rest of us. Chainlink dominates today, with estimates of up to 80% of all smart contracts making use of its services on any given day.

This makes Chainlink perhaps the most important player in DeFi, at least from the perspective of our maddeningly unpredictable world. That is no small achievement.

CHAPTER 12

Reinventing insurance – Nexus Mutual

I t turns out that the application of DeFi and smart contracts to the insurance sector is still constrained – the attack surface in the insurance sector is, perhaps temporarily, smaller than the banking and exchange examples we have seen previously.

Let's take a look at the insurance industry from the perspective of a consumer. You want to purchase cover for your new car. You call an insurance company, give the car's details, and your own, and get a quote. This quote represents a number that takes various factors into account – your car, you (as an individual: your accident history, age, address, etc.) and what you intend doing with the car (personal, business). All of this information is thrown into an actuarial washing machine somewhere in the bowels of the insurance company, and a number is thrown up. You are offered a certain cover for a certain term and subject to various conditions.

Insurance companies themselves have enormous legacy footprints that back up this service: actuarial armies, assessors with specific expertise (hang on, we'll cover this fender dent but not that scratch on the door) and a reinsurance sector that will insure the insurers. Not to mention a large pool of capital and credit to pay claims, even in the case of 'black swan' events like earthquakes.

And teams to make sure that everything conforms to the screeds of regulations. Oh, and the needs of shareholders to receive a return on investment.

It would be nice to report that a DeFi smart contract can insure your car. But it can't. That's because the birth of DeFi insurance was inward-looking, not outward-looking. It sought to cover risks within the crypto ecosystem. Not cars, houses, floods and earthquakes.

At least not yet.

Hugh Karp graduated as an actuary in Australia in 2001 and eventually found his way to London, a historical insurance centre with the venerable Lloyd's of London, formed in a coffee house in 1688, still standing proud. Karp joined the industry and worked his way up the insurance ladder until, like others in this story, he realised that a marriage of Ethereum's smart contracts and insurance could produce progeny that would outrun the stolid legacy companies, even with their massive capital pools, global brands and entrenched legacies.

Karp chewed on this idea for a while, watching with increasing excitement as DeFi apps started to line up and launch. While everyone was innovating in finance applications, no one was grabbing the insurance opportunity. Perhaps because at the centre of insurance is risk, and risk is deeply understood mostly by actuaries, who are a rare breed indeed, with Actuarial Science a university degree only for the brave.

So he got together with another actuary he knew, Reinis Melbardis, and thought the problem through. Surely the power of blockchain and decentralisation and smart contracts would be tailor-made for insurance disruption? And so when they had the proposition bedded down they wrote a white paper for a new company called Nexus Mutual.

The introduction to this white paper makes for fascinating reading. In fact the whole paper glows with a deep understanding of insurance, well-reasoned arguments and strategic and tactical intent, at least until the maths gets dense enough for all but the most highly motivated.

The paper starts off with some historical context. Prior to the development of insurance companies, local communities took on the responsibility of mitigating shared risk. Community members contributed to a shared pool, from which funds were dispersed to individuals wounded by the slings and arrows of outrageous fortune. This practice continues in many places. In South Africa, for example, there are funeral societies which will pay for funerals from a community fund (funerals are often ostentatious affairs, far beyond the means of most rural people). Other schemes have senior members deciding on pay-outs for less predictable misfortunes than funerals.

Obviously, community schemes don't scale. When the number gets into the thousands and beyond, centralised institutionalisation starts to make sense. Insurance companies take premiums into a capital pool and pay out on valid claims. Which is where it gets more complicated. The underlying maths showed that by pooling many different sorts of risks, the capital pool could be used more efficiently. So when your car insurance premium goes in, it will be made available for pay-outs for other things – houses, floods, motorcycles, film bonds, key man insurance and anything else that your insurance company may choose to cover. They, of course, do not keep your premiums in a vault for a possible pay-out to you, or even in a vault with all the other car insurance premiums; much in the same way that banks use your deposit to facilitate loans out to anonymous others for a variety of purposes.

The authors of the paper articulate two problems. The first, which they call 'Agency', refers to the fact that the insurance company takes custody of your funds and gives you no right whatsoever to question what they do with it. Of course, they are imprisoned by thick walls of laws and regulation to prevent them from unduly gambling your money, but it is still opaque. Let's say the insurance company wants to start covering, say, weather risk for large outdoor events. That will likely be allowed by regulators, but your opinion as a customer of the insurance company doesn't count. Your premiums may well go to pay out to a claimant whose outdoor gospel concert was rained off. You also have no input on dividends to shareholders, or other investments the company may choose to make, like opening up in a new country where there may be entrenched competition.

The second problem, somewhat related, they call 'Transparency'. How safe is your insurance company? How well have they managed risk? This is extremely difficult to find out, even in public companies. They will not reveal this to you, a customer, or to the public at large.

Both of these scream the same problem – information asymmetry. We know little, they know all. It is the tracks on which these companies smoothly glide.

Karp launched Nexus Mutual in 2017. He was insistent on not having it seen as an insurance company, partly for legal reasons – insurance companies are among the most regulated entities in the world. He called it a peer-to-peer discretionary mutual, because mutuals are outside the rump of insurance regulations. It was a philosophical return to a community pool, where funds are held for the common good and protection is spread around. Or perhaps Karp was also trying to avoid the taint of old-world legacy insurance. But, language being what it is, Nexus Mutual is considered the first DeFi insurance company.

And since that launch (initially seed-funded, and later by the restricted sale of their NXM token), this DeFi company has taken a path that is, in important ways, different from the DeFi companies we have been discussing.

So how does Nexus Mutual work? In the earliest of incarnations, Karp actually tried (or at least thought about trying) to sell earthquake insurance via smart contract, but it quickly became apparent that the universe of DeFi users and the universe of people scared of earthquakes did not intersect much. So a quick pivot, and an identification of a risk area *within* DeFi which was crying out for risk mitigation, and that was smart contracts. Smart contracts are programs. Written by humans. Who are fallible and make mistakes. Those mistakes have famously resulted in the draining of funds from a number of projects by bad actors, or simply because the smart contract didn't work as intended and lost funds. The DAO, bZx, YAM and others come to mind.

This was the first Nexus Mutual product and it was immediately successful. A gremlin or vulnerability in a smart contract is not like leaving a window to a house open, giving a burglar an opportunity to nick some cell phones and the silverware. In smart contracts holding capital, hundreds of millions and more are potentially at stake.

More recent offerings from Nexus Mutual have included the insuring of protocols themselves, meaning entire end-to-end DeFi projects, like Compound. This includes oracle attacks, governance attacks and other increasingly arcane threats. Nexus Mutual now also covers the insurance of crypto-exchanges, which are the most frequently exploited attack vectors, being the gateway into underlying applications and historically the most vulnerable and appetising point-of-entry for hackers.

This created the first of many challenges, which was the enlistment of rare skills to audit and bless the inner workings of complex software running smart contracts and other applications. There are for-profit companies who offer this service, like OpenZeppelin and Trail of Bits. Rather than hiring one of these centralised businesses to assess and provide a stamp of health (these companies charge more than pretty pennies for their services), Nexus Mutual offers a public incentive. Anyone wishing to adjudicate the security risk of an underlying product stakes their NXM tokens against their expertise, and is rewarded when other members buy cover on the risks they stake against, and is punished if there is a claim on their risks. So the security assessors have a built-in incentive to do their job well – correctly analysing the risk of covered products would help Nexus Mutual avoid unnecessary pay-outs, thereby increasing the company's value, thereby increasing the value of the NXM tokens and increasing the quality of service to customers. The adjudicated risk on which the premium is based is thereby crowd-sourced by people with motive and means.

This is novel and without any precedent in traditional insurance. Imagine this from a legacy insurer: 'We call on all qualified people anywhere in the world to come and help us calculate risks for our product suite. If you get it right we will give you some stock in our company. If not, you pay us.'

Other people qualifying for NXM tokens are participants buying smart contract cover, or providing capital, or governing the protocol, or assessing claims. These entities, in keeping with the 'mutual' theme, are called members.

All of this means that in contrast to other DeFi projects we have discussed, incentives are not simply offered to the public to pump money into a liquidity pool. They are offered only to participants with (or who wish to have) a stake in the game. NXM tokens cannot be bought on a public exchange, they can only be acquired on the Nexus Mutual website on purchasing cover or being approved as a value-adding contributor in some other way. Furthermore, every NXM-holder is KYC'd (Know Your Customer requirements, IDs and the like), a shocking policy in a world where anonymity is prized. There are good reasons for this, all put in place to avoid running afoul of regulators.

A second difference from other DeFi projects is that Nexus Mutual is not a DAO, a Decentralised Autonomous Organisation, at least not yet. Nexus Mutual refers to itself as a Digital Cooperative. There is a core advisory team of five experts and founders who mediate and approve various matters. That would be a centralised *bête noire* redolent of old-world corporations and their boards, except that NXM token-holders can vote and replace members of this team. Representative democracy, again, also called delegated authority.

But Nexus Mutual does run into the problem of trustlessness in one important respect. There is not currently an automated way to adjudicate some claims. Let's say that an insured smart contract is exploited, and money is lost. The losers claim from Nexus Mutual. Now comes the hard part – how was the smart contract exploited? Was it hacked? Who hacked it? Was it neglect? Was it some contract developer's malfeasance? Was it an attack from a devious and brilliant external party who saw something no one else saw? These questions can only be answered by human expertise, and rare expertise at that. It is difficult to imagine a smart contract being able to assign cause and effect for loss in such a complex ecosystem of blockchains, contracts, mathematics, wallets and human action. It is where the utopian goals of trustlessness collapse under the weight of the complexity of real things. Smart contracts cannot do everything.

None of this invalidates the value of Nexus Mutual, though. There may be some grumbling from DeFi maximalists in that parts of its offering have to traffic outside of smart contracts. But we would argue that this is actually where the ground for innovation is most fertile – designing products that use the best of both worlds.

Nexus Mutual has put together an unusual offering, even by DeFi standards, which is novel in many respects. It is a mutual society made up of experts and funders and cover-seekers, all directly incentivised by the success of the 'mutual'. There is no information asymmetry, all participants know what is being done with the pool of capital, all know which crypto technologies are covered, and the front page of the Nexus Mutual website shows boldly and clearly how they are doing: $524m in active cover and $15m in annualised premiums at the time of writing. If enough mutual participants don't like how or what the company is doing, they can fire the advisory board and appoint a new one. This utterly overturns hundreds of years of formal insurance company policy.

$524m in active cover is a mere speck on the traditional insurance industry's vast canvas. Nexus Mutual and all their other competitors (like Etherisc, Cover, Opium and Evertas) are clearly not yet a threat to AXA, State Farm or Allianz. But consider this, from the Nexus Mutual white paper: 'Roughly 35% of traditional insurance premiums are lost due to frictional costs in the system. Only 65% of premiums are returned to customers via claims, the rest is lost in distribution, operational expenses (including regulatory), capital costs and profit.' Note that the last item, profit, does not mean the same thing in a mutual – all 'profits' belong to its members, who decide on how they are to be used, either to be deployed into the mutual, invested, or distributed.

Even if you ignore the benefits to customers from the collapsing of the information and power asymmetries facilitated by underlying DeFi technologies, just the operational savings available to the industry by shedding legacy systems and moving onto the blockchain alone are mouth-watering.

While the new players in this field are still finding their feet and building sustainable business, it will not be long before they turn to the coverage of physical-world assets like cars and houses and businesses, as well as the big targets of health and life insurance – finding ways to apply the concepts of decentralisation and trustlessness to them too.

This is inevitable, and probably closer than insurance executives think. DeFi is coming for the rest of this industry too.

CHAPTER 13

The scalability trilemma and its discontents

We now jump sideways to take a look at what the early DeFi successes and the continual sprouting of new DeFi projects have wrought. In short, the explosion of smart contracts and associated projects on Ethereum has brought so many transactions onto the network that it has started to groan under the weight. 'Gas' fees, which are the price of anyone using the network, have risen dramatically to levels that have made a mockery of early claims of Ethereum being a 'low transaction fee' ecosystem.

A visit to the Twittersphere will reveal much unhappiness and snark about this. But, on the other hand, and given the stakes, this has caused a flurry of invention, from entirely new blockchains with smart contract capability to brow-furrowing new parallel architectures using scary words like 'parachain' and 'relay chain', all trying to compete with the Ethereum blockchain. And then there are numerous projects and proposals to lighten Ethereum's load via removing some of the heavy lifting from the blockchain and depositing it somewhere else for processing before handing back its finished work to Ethereum – referred to as 'rollups' (covered later in this chapter).

Keeping our eye on the prize, we must remember what is happening here. In an astonishingly short time and in full view, we have seen the birth of a parallel monetary system and the beginnings of a new financial services system. The history of technology has rarely seen anything on this scale. From the printing press to electricity to motor vehicles to radios to TV to the PC to the Internet, nothing of this potential impact has moved anywhere this fast, the dollar volume of which bears repeating – from zero to around $2 trillion has been moved into cryptocurrencies in about ten years. Even the mobile phone, which saw the light of day in the mid-1990s, had to travel through more than two decades to get to where it is now.

The DeFi innovators grappling with engineering and technology and interface problems at the coalface are aware, even if subconsciously, of how impactful this could be, not merely in the frame of their lifetimes, but in the next five to ten years. So when the training wheels start to come off, as they are now, everyone knows that speed and throughput and cost of operation at the core technology layers are problems that have to be solved with urgency. It is not a matter for plodding bureaucracy or industry bodies; that takes too long. It has to be done now, even if the carcasses of once promising solutions are left to rot on the roadside. And there are already many of those.

We have continually made reference to the following three benefits of this new technology: security (tamper resistance), decentralisation (censorship resistance) and scalability (the ability to support an arbitrary number of transactions and users without noticeable degradation of performance).

Vitalik Buterin made a controversial claim in 2015, while still a teenager leading a very young Ethereum. He claimed that blockchains could not satisfy all three requirements equally. You could do two very well, but the third would suffer. So carefully choose what you want to optimise for. It was called the Trilemma Dilemma.

Buterin's opinion has caused furious debate (and software development, and not a few dense academic papers) in the intervening six years. There have been numerous 'We've solved it!' technologies, which on closer inspection have not, rather shifting around the trilemma hither and thither. But the trilemma has focused an enormous amount of brain power on the following problem: how can a technology architecture be built that sufficiently addresses the requirements of security, decentralisation and scalability in order to solve real-world problems?

What does 'sufficiently' mean? Here is an example. Let's say a blockchain had only one machine to validate a transaction. This is obviously a *reductio ad absurdum* proposition. This would mean that the blockchain was completely centralised, with all power in the hands of a single machine and its operator, who could be a bad actor. Now add one more anonymous machine to check the transaction. Still pretty centralised. Ten anonymous computers? Not bad, unless all ten machines get together in a cabal and change transactions to their benefit. One hundred anonymous computers? Better. One thousand? Better still. Two thousand? Wait. Is that any more decentralised than one thousand? Not so much. And there's the rub. How much decentralisation is enough?

Similar questions can be asked of network speed and throughput and cost – how fast is fast enough, how many transactions per unit time is enough, and what cost is bearable? Another example. If you want to pay for something online, you expect authorisation in seconds, your benchmark is credit card speed, and you want your fees to be manageable. But if you want to pay, settle and clear an important invoice, perhaps a few minutes would be fine, and you still would like fees to be small in relation to invoice amount. And for something larger, like payment for a sizeable international shipment of goods, perhaps you don't care if it stretches a bit longer, and if it is a million-dollar payment, transaction fees have a higher pain threshold.

Security, a different matter, refers to the level of defensibility a blockchain has against attacks from external sources. It is strong when protected by the encryption technologies we discussed earlier as applied to individual transactions, but there are other security threats: the 51% attack (meaning that entities conspire to control more than 50% of the network nodes, thereby owning the network), Sybil attacks (where one entity is actually secretly controlling many nodes, named after the book detailing the many schizophrenic personalities of a psychiatric patient named Sybil), denial of service attacks (clogging the network), etc. There are many of these.

This matter of 'sufficiency' has birthed its own phrase among academically-minded crypto researchers. It has been branded 'weak subjectivity'. As in – yeah, that seems good enough to me. Secure enough for me, or fast enough for me, inexpensive enough for me.

DeFi developers have an urgent stake in these matters. The slower the network is, and more pointedly, the higher the fees are, the more it leads to user resistance. All DeFi projects measure their success by number of users, particularly where liquidity is the engine that feeds them, so any friction in that regard is a threat. This leg of the trilemma, scalability, is what most DeFi stakeholders care about.

And so a great race is underway. Handicapping turns out to be difficult – there is a surfeit of very clever people researching and developing possible solutions to the scalability problem, and working as though the future of the business depends on it. Which, in a sense, it does. Bitcoin always settles a block in about ten minutes; this is built into Satoshi's design. It can therefore never be both a fast payment and settling instrument, unless it is entirely re-engineered (fast BTC payment has indeed been enabled by some clever solutions, the best known of which is Lightning, discussed below). Ethereum settles blocks of transactions at a rate of about fifteen transactions per second. This is much faster than Bitcoin, but still slow next to, say, the Visa credit card system which can process tens of thousands of transactions per second (although with delayed settlement). Ethereum fees are also often over $50 per transaction, depending on network load, and sometimes considerably more, having exceeded $500 per transaction in a volatile period in May 2021, killing the prospect of all but the larger, non-retail transactions. A workable scalability solution would be, as they say, the killer app.

Some jargon is now inescapable. Blockchains like Bitcoin and Ethereum are known as Layer 1. They are the base plumbing, more formally called the base consensus layer, articulated by what we have called the 'protocol' that describes them. This base plumbing is used to move tokens securely from wallet to wallet. In Ethereum's case, it is under the control of a computer program, a smart contract, written by somebody offering a service on the blockchain. And it is slow, at least relative to the rising expectations of its users.

In this way Bitcoin, Ethereum and other blockchains are information networks that conform to the same typology as the Internet. There is a base protocol – TCP/IP in the case of the Internet – and then there are application protocols that are layered on top of it, which is the stuff users actually see.

One solution to the scalability problem is to develop a better blockchain, a better Layer 1 or base protocol; a faster consensus layer. Even if it means compromising one of the sides of the scalability trilemma triangle. There is Binance Smart Chain, which is basically a copy of Ethereum with fewer nodes, meaning lower decentralisation, meaning greater throughput. There is Solana, whose solution mandates much faster and more powerful computers to run nodes, which because of their cost (about $3,500) has the effect of reducing decentralisation, given that fewer people can afford expensive validation nodes. The higher-spec computers also have the intended advantage of speeding up the actual compute tasks on the nodes. Most of Ethereum's nodes run on inexpensive off-the-shelf computers, and this is how it was intended – whereas a $3,500 computer will produce orders of magnitude increases in speed. Solana's solution thus improves scalability by sacrificing decentralisation. And then there are other flavours of new Layer 1 blockchains including Polkadot, Cardano, Stellar, Cosmos and others, each offering speeds that are considerably faster than Ethereum and fees that are considerably lower, plus new fancy functions that make crypto technologists salivate – although it must be said that they also transfer but a fraction of the value and code processed on Ethereum. One can always travel faster on a highway that no one else is using. Time will tell if they have truly cracked the problem.

All of these players, to a greater or lesser extent, face formidable challenges in trying to unseat Ethereum. The first is that in its approximately seven years of existence, Ethereum has assembled by far the largest and arguably the smartest developer pool in the cryptosphere. They are all aware of the scaling problem, they have not been sitting still. Secondly, Ethereum has hosted over a million smart contracts, and currently hosts the most mature of the DeFi projects which transact billions of dollars daily. To be fair, some of the new Layer 1 blockchains can run Ethereum-compatible contracts without much change, like BSC. But DeFi projects would prefer that Ethereum could find a way to solve the problem itself, as there is simply more weight and prestige behind the pioneer of smart contract architectures. Developers can call upon functions in the millions of smart contracts already on Ethereum. The box of legos on newer chains is empty; on Ethereum, the toolset is vast.

DeFi smart contract developers don't want to be part of a Layer 1 war, they just want a single winner, and speed and economy. Like the Internet, nobody wants a second one. Except China, perhaps.

In fact Ethereum itself (meaning the core wizards in an organisation called the Ethereum Foundation) has indeed put its shoulder to the Layer 1 wheel, with a number of new approaches submitted by the Ethereum community having been accepted and carefully developed and now in the middle of a rollout schedule, collectively known as Ethereum 2.0, 'Serenity', or its more abbreviated Eth2. The upgrades being implemented are technically arcane, but again, the principle is not.

There are two major Layer 1 improvements in Eth2. The first is not a new concept, having been used in computer science for decades. It is called sharding, where a database is broken up into a subset of smaller databases for processing. This is implemented in Eth2, where transaction data requiring validation from a particular block is broken up into 64 shards, and sent to 64 'child' blockchains for processing. Each one being fast and inexpensive.

There were a number of safeguards that had to be developed to maintain the security arm of the trilemma in doing this.

Importantly, with 64 child blockchains, someone has to coordinate all of them. This is called the Beacon Chain, which is the conductor of the whole sharding operation. It is, in effect, a move to parallel processing. This is a non-trivial change: development work has been going on for years, and theoretically it should scale the network a thousand-fold, although in practice it is likely to be less; it will not be clear until the system is working in production. An unscientific poll of articles and opinions online predicts that transactions will go from fifteen per second to somewhere around 5,000 per second, taking the ecosystem to within range of credit card transaction speed.

The second major Layer 1 chain upgrade is in the way that nodes are rewarded for validating transactions. Traditionally miners have done this via a scheme called Proof-of-Work, which is compute-intensive and has therefore been the subject of much unhappiness in a carbon-footprint-conscious world. Eth2 will see a move to a 'node validator' reward system called Proof-of-Stake, both more energy-efficient and faster than Proof-of-Work, in which nodes stake some ETH currency and are chosen randomly to do the validation. Miscreants lose their stake, successful validators will get a reward, which is how honesty is incentivised. So instead of using compute power to earn your rights on the network, in Eth2 you pay for them instead.

Which brings us to the battlefield that is Layer 2. This refers to a slew of projects across the crypto space that have implemented (or are busy implementing) solutions to helpfully take some of the heavy compute tasks off the Layer 1 network and process them on a second layer, which is built upon Layer 1, and, critically, inherits the security from the base layer.

One of the most famous of these Layer 2s was first proposed on the Bitcoin blockchain. It is called Lightning and allows near-instantaneous BTC payments between participating parties on the Bitcoin network via a set of Lightning-specific 'payment channels', without having to wait for the tortuous ten-minute block-processing time. It is operational, works well, and is finding an increasing number of users. Similar Layer 2 solutions are underway to help out Ethereum, currently exhausted from overuse. Some of these Layer 2 solutions are being orchestrated by the Ethereum Foundation itself under the multi-phase Eth2 project.

All Layer 2 solutions are, as in Layer 1, deep into the weeds of computer science. The majority of them use one of a number of flavours of what are called rollups. In short, transactions are bundled together, moved up to Layer 2 and then returned to Layer 1 after execution. This is different from the data sharding discussed earlier for Layer 1, in that these transactions are processed 'off-chain' in Layer 2. This will again bump the speed of transaction processing, perhaps to as high as 100,000 transactions per second. Eth2's schedule to deliver all of these pieces of the puzzle, including some we haven't mentioned, will be sometime early in 2022, although there are phased releases along the way, with fancy and inscrutable names like Altair, London and Merge.

We are painfully aware that details of all this 'make it faster and cheaper' scaling technology are subtle, complex and difficult for non-crypto developers to fully comprehend. It feels a little like trying to understand particle physics – unless the underlying mathematics is fully understood, it remains somewhat blurred.

One should also consider the predictable progress of any new technology, particularly where information networks are concerned. In the early days of consumer Internet adoption it would take many hours just to download a small file at speeds measured in bits-per-second. The thought of transferring large image files was preposterous, let alone streaming high-definition video.

Those less familiar with network science saw this as a critical impediment to the Internet ever being used for anything more than email and viewing simple websites. Information scientists knew better. It was an engineering problem, nothing else. By scaling the Internet through protocols such as HTTP and codecs that made everything from telephony to streaming video possible, the Internet grew incrementally at first and then exponentially thanks, in no small part, to Metcalfe's Law, which states that 'the value of a telecommunications network is proportional to the square of the number of connected users of the system'. Put simply: the more people use a network, the more useful it becomes to everyone else using it, in an exponential way.

Had we thrown up our hands at the assumed limitations in throughput of the Internet in the 1990s we would have been deprived of the wonders of Netflix and Google today. Instead we kept adding to the network until its scaling problems were solved.

Such is the pressure to solve the scaling problem in cryptocurrency, and given the financial value that will be unlocked by fast, low-fee DeFi, that we found the following companies all chasing the same 'speed up Ethereum' rainbow: Optimistic, Abitrum, Fuel Network, Loopring, StarkWare, Aztec, Matter Labs, OMG Network, Matic Network, Gazelle, Leap DAO, Connext, Raiden, Perun. And of course, Ethereum's own efforts.

These comprise the best minds in the business. This problem will be solved.

CHAPTER 14

Derivatives

The sharp-eyed reader will have noticed that everything that has been described so far has been about tokens and coins, whether it be Bitcoin (BTC) or Ether (ETH) or any number of the other currencies or governance tokens or utility tokens that have made an appearance in the preceding pages. The connection with the real world has really only been two-fold – exchanging tokens for real dollars, and using oracles to communicate with the outside world. Smart contracts and Solidity and other contract programming languages enable the movement of tokens between addresses on blockchain under a set of specified conditions, nothing else. The value of the tokens floats innocently, made concrete by the magic of the free market, where traders make decisions as to market price by buying and selling. One exception to this is the stablecoin, by design firmly rooted to the value of a real currency, but 'tokenised' for easy commercial intercourse with other tokens.

But what of stocks and bonds? Commodities? Options? Futures and swaps? To what extent is crypto trespassing there?

A lot, as it happens.

Let's return to the 'quadrillion dollars' in the chapter on oracles. This is the total value of the global derivatives market, which is over ten times the size of all global stock markets. What is a derivative, exactly? It is simply a value derived from the current price of an asset. So the price of gold now may not be the value of gold three months from now. A futures contract is built around what it is believed the price will be hence. It is 'derived' from today's price. If you believe in the upward movement of the price of oil, you do not actually have to buy and take delivery of barrels of oil, but may choose to purchase an *option* to sell at a particular price which you predict at a later date. The option price is derived from the price of oil. The best-known assets with derivative offspring are stocks, bonds, commodities and interest rates, although there is no in-principle restriction on what else can be used, as long as there is a market for the derivative instrument. The best-known derivatives products are forwards, futures, options and swaps, but there are numerous more exotic creatures, some with underlying maths so obtuse as to be understood only by a few, and famously and derisively referred to by Warren Buffett as financial 'kryptonite'. Almost all derivatives, however, are time-based, and depend on some future event or date, and derive their value from a currently priced asset.

Derivatives are a feature of any mature financial system and they are certainly not new – Sumerian clay tablets from 8000 BCE have indicated a 'forwards' market, promises to deliver goods in the future based on a current price. Futures markets to hedge crop prices were well developed in Japan and Europe in medieval times, and in the US the Chicago Board of Trade, the first derivatives market, started in 1848.

Why would anyone buy a derivative? By far the most common usage of the derivative is as a hedge against future nastiness. Bad weather, if you are a farmer. An adverse change in your country's currency in relation to another, if you are an importer or exporter. A change in interest rates if you are a financier. In a larger sense, derivatives are a mechanism for selling peace of mind to commercial actors – for a fee, you get predictable and long-term stability of value. This is only one of the derivative market's two audiences, but it comprises a huge population of participants seeking regulated and formalised risk mitigation, and it is well traded and useful in a world where, as we mentioned, shit happens.

The second group of traders are speculators. They are not seeking to protect the ramparts of any commercial enterprise, but have a much simpler mission – to bet on the future price of assets, using whatever intelligence or data or intuitions they have at hand, and to profit off the commercial actors who have an opposite opinion. Speculators are on the other side of the trade to the hedgers, and provide the ever-important liquidity to make the market work.

The derivatives market is also dangerous, as the public has been reminded many times. It is common practice to borrow, or leverage, in order to control a larger stake than what is deposited. If the price moves in your direction, you get huge profits, but if not, liquidation of your deposit can happen quickly.

The people who have traditionally worked in derivatives, particularly the wizards who build and test the products with ingeniously modelled mathematical harnesses, are famously smart. They can be found in the warrens of the large financial institutions, sporting advanced degrees from big universities and earning eye-watering salaries. It is no surprise that some of these people watched the rise of DeFi and jumped aboard, understanding well how large and fast DeFi derivatives could grow from this small base. And some have come from outside of finance, bringing new eyes to an old stage.

And so there has been a swarm of DeFi derivative projects. One of them is Synthetix, with a market capitalisation of over $6bn, making it one of the largest DeFi projects. But Synthetix started reasonably far from the future-triggered derivatives of TradFi. Perhaps this was because Kain Warwick, the Sydney-based founder, came from a retail and retail-based payments background as opposed to the corporate financial sector. In any event, his frustration with retail payment systems led to an early attempt to build a stablecoin. Other stablecoins beginning their life were accepted more readily by the market, so Synthetix decided to pivot. Pivot, for those unfamiliar with the euphemism, is a new millennium word that basically means, 'We failed, gonna do something else now.' Where they saw the gap was that certain assets were untradable in the world of crypto. Commodities, for instance. Stocks. Currencies (other than the dollar, well represented by DAI and Tether and other stablecoins).

So they had a very simple idea. Ask people to put their money (via ETH or BTC, for instance) into a Synthetix pool, called a debt pool – much like a staked liquidity pool, with obligations owed to the stakers. Each liquidity provider would be provided SNX tokens to the value of what was contributed (SNX itself has a value decided by the market – it is tradable on various DEXs). The SNX token could then be provided to a 'minter', called Mintr, which would 'mint' sXAU (synthetic gold) or sTESLA (synthetic Tesla stock) or sOIL (synthetic oil) and so on, depending on what is needed by the trader. And here is the nub – the price of all these synthetic assets, or 'Synths', is exactly the same as they are in the real world, whose prices are provided continuously by the helpful external oracles discussed earlier, like Chainlink's oracle network. The Synths' prices are *derived* from the underlying assets. They are pure derivatives.

Why, you may ask, would anyone do this? Because it allowed crypto traders to make trades on the price of underlying assets in the real world. You might not own the TESLA stock, might not get dividends and circulars from the company, but you would be exposed to its price. Without Synthetix, any crypto trader of a mind to take a position on a commodity or stock or bond would have to go back to real life, and sign in to a traditional stock exchange or derivatives market and use real fiat currency to make the trade. That world of traditional trading assets and DeFi did not intersect at all before Synthetix. Now all trades for this growing list of assets (which includes both multiple real-world assets and other crypto-currencies) can be executed in the same place, from a highly liquid pool, without the need for an order book, and most importantly, without the need for an account.

There are a number of wrinkles that we haven't discussed, to avoid a bog-down, such as the need for liquidity contributors to over-collateralise the debt pool contribution to protect against price swings, liquidity and staking incentives offered, commission/fee sharing, and the DAO governance mechanisms, but these are not too far removed from those that have been discussed previously in other projects. And, importantly and uniquely, Synthetix has the ability to trade shorts as well as longs (short selling is betting that a price will go down, a well-known but sophisticated tool of investors looking for profits in both up and down markets), announced in early 2021, providing a critical tool for savvy investors.

The derivatives cat was out of the bag, and so a number of other players dove in, some of them with products that looked closer to the elaborate products back at Goldman Sachs.

An example of this is Hegic, launched in October 2020. They are in the business of options, which gives the option-holder the right, but not the obligation, to buy or sell an asset at a set price some time in the future (known as 'call' and 'put' options, respectively). Their first products allow the buying and selling of calls and puts for ETH and BTC. The details of options trading are well known to professional traders in TradFi, and it is a specialist business with its own jargon like 'strike prices' and 'in-the-money' and 'option-writers'. Hegic was developed by an anonymous woman (presumably) named 'Molly Wintermute', but clearly someone with deep experience in how options work on traditional exchanges. One person, developing an entire options trading ecosystem on Ethereum. In months, not years or decades.

Hegic has lifted most of the well-known inner mathematical and economic workings of traditional options and has dropped them into a smart contract, allowing the application of the options trading instrument to both Ether and Bitcoin (with more crypto assets to come). We should note that options in TradFi are, like all derivatives, heavily regulated. A trader needs to be 'accredited' and prove some level of minimum financial health and sign disclaimers and indemnities of various kinds. This makes it difficult for a small retail investor to play in the options market – again displaying the basic asymmetry in the accessibility of traditional finance. With Hegic anyone gets to play. No ID, no KYC, no minimum amount. They can buy or sell calls or puts, or stake capital into the liquidity pools that underwrite the 'writing' of options that are traded.

To give a further taste of what is going on in derivative innovation in DeFi, we'll take a quick sprint through some of the activity in this space, which barely existed a year previously. There is UMA, which looks a little like Synthetix but uses no oracles (which are corruptible, in principle), rather employing the more human technique of rewarding anyone who spots someone who has become under-collateralised, and liquidating them. Token-holders are like guards, who can instantly check the blockchain (via any one of many public sources) to find out who is in trouble with their investment, and busting them to the authorities. This technique allows application of derivatives to assets not yet listed on big exchanges with trustworthy oracle-ready price feeds (of which there are many), so it has a potentially really wide footprint of new crypto offerings. It is a self-governing system without the need for oracles, who are only called in when there is a dispute.

There is Perpetual Protocol and other similar initiatives all offering what have come to be known as 'perps', products similar to traditional futures and options, but in which there is no contract termination date – the contract lasts for ever until the trader exits. This is not possible in TradFi, and is funded by the pool of long traders and short traders betting against each other, and an ingenious pricing mechanism for keeping stability in the trading pool and associated derivatives.

There is dYdX, a veteran of this young business, offering a suite of derivative products, from margins to options to perps.

There is Barnbridge, whose range of products hedge against volatility in various yield-producing instruments.

And more of these exotics are unveiled on a monthly, and sometimes weekly basis.

Andre Cronje from Yearn, on a call with the authors during this book's research, commented drily that 'DeFi is banking for geeks. TradFi is banking for bankers.'

Given the thicket of exotic choices and options glimpsed in the preceding pages, one needs to ask the obvious question. If DeFi is banking for geeks and TradFi is banking for bankers, then what is banking for the rest of us? Perhaps a better analogy would be the march of previous but recent technologies: the Internet, the smart-phone, the rise of apps. There were geeks all over the development of these technologies too, until people with other skills found out a way to make them easy to use. As easy as the Uber app, behind which is hidden multiple technologies from GPS to payment gate-ways to map applications to data science.

Derivatives represent perhaps the most arcane of the DeFi apps covered so far. But underneath it all remains the simplest of aspirations – how is money best put to use in the service of its owner? We contend that two things need to be solved. The creaky and inaccessible machinery of TradFi needs to be re-imagined and re-implemented, which is what is clearly underway here, and then the social designers need to fashion an interface for users that hides the complexity underneath.

This is inevitable. There are trillions riding on that. Of course the heady days of 100%+ yields and thousands of percent appre-ciation in the price of governance tokens must one day end. At that point we will be left with a more flexible, less expensive, more accessible and fairer financial system. And the inventors who built some of these early engines will likely be tinkering with some-thing else.

CHAPTER 15

NFTs – beyond WTF

NFTs, which stands for non-fungible tokens, had an unfortunate public birth.

On March 11th, 2021, news outlets around the world breathlessly reported the $69m sale of the artist Beeple's *Everydays: The First 5000 Days* as an NFT-certified digital creation. The work itself was started in 2007. It consists of 5,000 small digital artworks, most of them depicting public figures and cultural memes, laid out as a single digital image. It is one of the highest prices paid for a piece of art in history.

Public opinion was swift and brutal. Few people knew what an NFT was. Most only knew that it was a fancy new technology that seemed to fuel shocking sticker prices for digital art, including art that seemed to some to be, er, mediocre. But you could hear disbelieving conversations at gyms, restaurants and stores for days after, not to mention flames coming out of social media. $69 million? For thousands of little digital thumbnails smooshed together into a big picture? What's the world coming to? And who owns this company called NFT?

The Beeple artwork was not the first, but its price made it the most public. An Andy Warhol computer image from the

1980s sold for \$870,000. A viral 'Charlie Bit My Finger' video on YouTube sold for \$760,999. The founder of Twitter, Jack Dorsey, sold his first tweet for \$2.9m. In 2017 a very basic digital drawing of a cat called Dragon, from the Ethereum game *CryptoKitties*, sold for \$170,000.

Perhaps one of the oddest stunts was on March 3rd, 2021, a week before the Beeple sale, when a group called the Injective Protocol, who had bought a Banksy artwork for \$95,000, attached an Ethereum-based NFT certificate of ownership to it and then burned the artwork on YouTube (with the added tension of the tiny lighter being used by the masked burner mightily struggling for a minute or two to get the canvas in flames). The NFT later sold at three times the amount of the original artwork purchase. The NFT is a secure certificate of ownership of the memory of a piece of art.

But it was only with the Beeple artwork auction one week later that the lid blew off the NFT industry, accompanied by a lot of noise from both the public square and ivory towers of academia.

What in the world was this thing, and more importantly, what did it mean for the future? And more to the concerns of this book, what does it mean for DeFi? To get to the root of this question we travel back to 2013, after Bitcoin, but before Ethereum. The original Bitcoin developers implementing the details of Satoshi's white paper had allowed the option to provide 'metadata', meaning extra data besides the details of the transaction, including data about data. For instance, the very first Bitcoin block, called the Genesis block, had the following text embedded: 'The Times 03/Jan/2009 Chancellor on brink of second bailout for banks', the significance of which has been pored over by crypto-historians. Transactions could also have extra data besides the critical transaction data, and a number of people started wondering if anything useful could be done with this spare data space.

Which brings us to the word 'fungible'. Meaning 'mutually interchangeable'. A ten euro note is fungible. Yours and mine can be exchanged, and we still each have the same ten euros to spend. An airplane ticket is non-fungible. You cannot use mine, because my name is on it. A Picasso original is also non-fungible. It is unique.

Bitcoin is fungible. One Bitcoin is the same as another. The people who were sniffing around new uses of the Bitcoin architecture in 2013, which included Vitalik Buterin, wondered whether there couldn't be different 'types' of Bitcoin, which were restricted to only certain uses. A name was adopted: Colored Coins. A colour for that sort of restricted Bitcoin class, a colour for this sort of restricted Bitcoin class. They listed possible classes – property, electronic access, stocks, contracts, specialist currencies, collectibles, subscriptions, reward coupons – and set to work implementing the Colored Coins on top of the Bitcoin network.

But alas. The Bitcoin architecture was not really designed for multiple use-cases beyond the single token. It was indeed possible to do, but clumsy and difficult to implement and maintain, given the tools available. This didn't stop a company called CounterParty from launching Colored Coin-like tokens and allowing exchangeability, but it was not an easy ride; it was before its time. CounterParty still exists, its $XCP still trades, but its market capitalisation is stuck in the also-ran doldrums of sub $10m. But the idea of the Colored Coin, the first approximation to an NFT, remained, gathering strength on Ethereum where it was eventually developed and published as another standard Ethereum protocol.

Before we continue with the story of NFTs and see their progression into DeFi, we need to get back to what an NFT is now, rather than the early attempts on the Bitcoin blockchain. If just a few words are required, we could say it is a *secured certification of ownership*. Like cryptographically secured. The strongest certificate of ownership on earth. But that is not quite enough, so we'll try to tighten the definition.

Firstly, every NFT is unique and uniquely distinguishable.

Secondly, it cannot be subdivided like a Bitcoin, which can be traded in amounts down to tiny fractions.

Thirdly, it must be provably scarce, akin to the limited numbered prints made by an artist.

Fourthly, just like any other token on blockchain, it must be transferable by permission of the owner, and secure. As an example, consider an NFT-registered ownership of reserved season seats in a stadium – there are only that many seats. Such an NFT would be identical for all stadium seats, but each would have a different *property*, that of the seat number.

And finally, each NFT on the blockchain always has an owner, verifiable and public.

So an NFT token on the Ethereum network proves ownership of something. Of what? Let's start with the easy stuff. A digitisable asset – a work of digital art, an item in a videogame, a video, a contract, an access code, a title deed – anything that can be digitised. Because once it is in digital form, cryptography can be used to create a 'digital fingerprint' of the asset, a small string of numbers sometimes called a digital signature, unique to the digital asset, which is attached to the NFT. So the NFT is incontrovertibly tied to some unique digital thing. No counterfeiting possible, courtesy of the one-way function and cryptography. Moreover, an NFT can be traded and sold freely on one of many online NFT markets like OpenSea or Rarible. Your piece of digital landscape art for my latest MP3 song, that sort of thing. Or your digital landscape art for my fungible ETH.

And it gets better. Because we are in the world of Ethereum and smart contracts, we can create rules and conditions. We'll mention just two powerful examples. The first goes like this: 'If this NFT is sold by seller A to buyer B for an agreed price of X ETH, then send 5% of that price to the address C.' Meaning that the creator of an artwork, who owns 'address C', can instruct their NFT to enforce continuing royalties on resold original work for ever, which does not occur with current real-world private sales of artworks or books or other privately owned creative treasures. Billions of dollars in resale revenue will automatically be delivered back to the original creators' wallets. That's a big pot of gold, unimaginable today, and a potentially game-changing financial landscape for art and talent.

And another example: an expensive artwork, like a Monet or Lucian Freud, can be sliced into 1,000 NFT pieces and sold to 1,000 investors, each piece at a fraction of the cost of the whole. Of course, no one gets to own enough of it to hang it on their wall, but artworks are as much investments as personal possessions. And each owner of that tiny piece of art gets to trade their fractional ownership at will. The TradFi industry can do this too, via a lawyer-heavy process called securitisation which is cooked up in arcane corners of the investment banking world. But not with the simplicity and elegance and openness and certainty of NFTs and smart contracts.

Notwithstanding the use-cases that were foreseen in the original white papers around Colored Coins and later NFT standards, markets have a way of deciding on where a technology will land. And videogaming is a big one, using NFTs to purchase cute animals in the game *CryptoKitties*, or avatars and tools in games like

Alien Worlds in order to use them in the game to win more often, or alternatively to sell them at a higher price to a more motivated player. Then there is *Decentraland*, a sort of hybrid game/world in which not only can players build and sell houses and other structures, they can also lease out advertising space to both real and virtual companies on the structure's wall or roof. This melds together the real and virtual worlds in mutant and unprecedented ways – real money and virtual money being paid for virtual real estate which can sport billboards advertising real products from real companies. NFTs have found a home there too, given that 'certifiable ownership' becomes non-negotiable when there is real money in the picture.

How big is the market, and where are NFTs being bought and sold and traded? One of the authoritative sources of data on this is a site called nonfungible.com which tracks these sorts of things. It lists primary NFT sales by value, NFT resales, number of NFTs sold, on which site/game/marketplace the sales happened and so on. The numbers are volatile – daily sales of both primary and secondary NFTs range from a low of about $10m to a high of $170m, with the mean being close to $60m. Number of sales, both primary and secondary, averages around 30,000 per day. And active wallets, meaning NFT owners, averages about 15,000 people or entities, at least on a quick visual scan of the charts. More interesting is that in 2020 there was almost nothing – few NFTs, few purchases, little dollar volume. Until late January 2021, when the industry suddenly seemed to catch fire, perhaps for the very reasons described in the opening of this chapter – somebody paid how much for what? WTF? Newspaper headlines!

A scan of the top sites selling and using NFTs is instructive. Out of the top twenty NFT purveyors at the time of writing we find these: CryptoPunks (digital artwork), Sorare (soccer trading cards), Meebits (digital artworks), The Sandbox (virtual building on virtual land), Art Blocks (computer-generated artworks seeded by the NFT owner). Then more digital art, more sporting collectibles, more virtual land and building projects. And a whole lot of loyalty tokens being awarded along the way for the purchase of these NFTs, which can be used or traded on public DEXs or reinvested in other pools that provide returns. We've seen this movie before in other projects in previous chapters. This is simply the gamification of established DeFi projects.

It is worth expanding on CryptoPunks' story. In 2017 two Canadian programmers, John Watkinson and Matt Hall of Larva Labs, both fans of the 'cyberpunk' movement of author William Gibson (whose book *Neuromancer* had become iconic in the movement) and movies like *Johnny Mnemonic* and *Blade Runner*, decided to build an automatic character generator for fun. It made very small blocky pixelated faces, 24×24 pixels in size, some with beanies, or earrings, or glasses. Importantly, they created a 'hash' – a unique digital signature – of the 10,000 characters created and gave them away. This meant that the CryptoPunks could not be digitally copied – they were unique. It was the inspiration for the development of the NFT smart contract rules (a standard now called ERC-721), which was developed shortly thereafter. Punk #7804, a guy with sunglasses smoking a blocky pipe, sold for $7.5m one day before the Beeple sale.

One of the most fascinating developments in the world of NFTs was a videogame that caught fire in 2021, when NFTs first emerged into popular consciousness. *Axie Infinity* was developed in Vietnam way back in 2018, and resembles the older analogue *Pokémon* game from a previous era.

The game itself requires three things to play. A prospective player needs three 'Axies' (cute little round characters) to join the game. In order to acquire these 'Axies', you have to buy them. Each Axie has its own NFT, and there is a marketplace for these, where they can be bought and sold. Once you are in the game you can create more cute characters by 'breeding', if you are good enough. Again, each newly bred Axie has its own NFT, which can then be traded.

So Axies then. To be used purely for in-game entertainment, or as an NFT investment to make real money on the crypto market where they can be sold. And here is what happened, starting in the Philippines, riddled with painful pandemic-caused unemployment. Players quickly realised that if they were good enough at the game, they could breed new Axies, and trade NFTs and make money. In fact, more money than in a regular job (at least a low-level job, like waitering). And a whole new economy quickly arose – *Axie Infinity* players making their living from playing and trading Axie NFTs (players can also buy and sell virtual real estate).

There are now over one million players worldwide, having spread beyond the Philippines to Indonesia and Venezuela. It is not unusual for players to make $2,000 per month and more, which can provide a reasonable living in those countries.

And then, to add to this strange new world, Andreessen Horowitz, the prestigious US-based tech investment company, provided capital to a collective called Yield Guild, who gather the best *Axie Infinity* players together and stake their entrance to the game in return for a cut of earnings. The guild members (called 'scholars') play, breed, quest, battle and trade their NFTs and make money. This is an economic activity that did not exist a mere few years ago and is certainly a harbinger of things to come.

One may be tempted to scoff at the dominance of the digital collectible market as the foundations on which NFTs have built their first home, until we consider that the global physical collectible market is $370bn, and the videogame market is $170bn, larger than film and music combined. And the values being put on some of these items may seem, well, frothy, but it is simply some person placing a value on an intangible creative asset. Humans have done this throughout history; it should not draw negative judgement.

Of course, the question becomes – when does this technology move from the world of games and collectibles and into the real world? We have a secure token of ownership called an NFT, with some distinguishing properties that can be defined, and smart contracts with which to attach conditions and caveats to the NFT, if so designed. Surely there are uses beyond games, sports trading cards and virtual real estate?

Number 13 on the top NFT list from the tracking site nonfungible .com (as we write this page) is the first to have functionality outside of these use-cases. It is the Ethereum domain service. It allows anyone to sign up with a '.ETH' domain, and have it lodged as uniquely owned, courtesy the properties of an NFT. Why would one use this? Well, it allows all those pesky, long, inscrutable wallet addresses, private keys, pass phrases and other information in the cryptosphere and beyond to be gathered in one place on the Ethereum blockchain. It is the uber password manager – a single '.ETH' address containing all other critical cryptographic and other access keys needed to navigate securely through the virtual world. And, as importantly, because it is on the Ethereum blockchain it is demonstrably secure and allows frictionless and tamper-proof interaction between your own I-AM-ME.ETH domain name and all other smart contracts on the blockchain. To give a feel for the worth of some of the NFT-certified EFT domain names, consider that 'EXCHANGE.ETH' is worth north of $500,000 per annum.

So let's continue down the NFT use-case path. Let's assume that an NFT is attached to the digitised title deed to your home. Through the magic of oracles, the NFT can update the value of your title deed daily, by accessing real-estate prices in your neighbourhood and interest rates and other key real-world data. Or returning to our NFT-certified sports trading cards, one can use oracles to update weekly statistics for the players, giving the cards the dynamic value that their static paper-based equivalents never had.

And here we arrive at the value that NFTs can bring to some of the DeFi projects discussed in previous chapters. The examples described below were taken from a terrific website called Finematics, whose videos about all matters DeFi are a marvel of reducing complexity to simplicity.

We have talked a lot about liquidity pools and automated market makers, those big pots of cash that enable smooth asset trading or loaning and lending of investor funds. The pools use incentives of one type or another to get investors to support the pool, ranging from interest to governance tokens. If an investor decides to contribute to a pool, they transfer their cryptocurrency – DAI or ETH or whatever, depending on the DeFi app and its currency acceptance policies.

Might these pools also accept NFTs as value-based contributions?

Let's assume that you were the sole owner of a Miró painting, whose agents had decided to certify your ownership via NFT. Let's say the Miró had a market worth of $1m. Given that a piece of art's value is not stable, but probably fairly predictable for a Miró, it is possible that the pool might accept the NFT to a value of $500,000, just in case there is an economic collapse and the value of all art plummets. This is called the loan-to-value amount in TradFi. So you would have just staked $500,000 of your painting's value into a pool which will deliver returns to you, and all the while still being able to enjoy the painting on your wall. To put it more simply, you have borrowed cryptocurrency against the real value of your painting and invested it in an interest-bearing crypto token. Where it can stay for ever, if you like, continuing to grow. This would be an unprecedented financial opportunity for millions of people. Usually, the only asset available for extracting value against is a house or other property, moreover only one that is largely or completely paid up. And it requires, as anyone who has remortgaged a home will know, a pile of paperwork and anxious waiting, to say nothing of fee upon fee.

Of course, the flaw here is that not everyone owns a house, much less a famous work of art. But there is an ingenious solution to this: peer-to-peer loans, enabled by another class of DeFi lender projects. Let's say you own a piece of digital art, which you have bought for 2 ETH via an NFT marketplace like OpenSea, from a real site such as CryptoPunks. You can go to a peer-to-peer lending site, and basically say – who will lend me 2 ETH for this piece of art?

If there are any takers (digital art aficionados, for instance, who understand this sort of stuff, and regularly collect), they will put your NFT into a smart contract escrow account, and send you 2 ETH. You put your ETH into anything you please – another liquidity pool or AMM which pays interest and other incentives, or a bet on a cryptocurrency price, or a vacation to Tahiti. You pay interest for the loan on the peer-to-peer platform. If you fail to pay your interest, the escrow contract transfers the ownership of the NFT to the peer-to-peer lender.

What we have just described is little more than a crypto pawn shop. The shop takes your grandmother's gold ring, gives you some cash, and holds the ring until you return the cash with interest. A tawdry business, as we learn from many films and TV shows. But with DeFi and NFTs, it is a potentially new way to unlock billions in stranded capital, a way for ordinary people to put small assets to work for them. A new DeFi project called NFTfi is currently providing this very service where borrowers post NFT-secured items and lenders decide on whether to make a loan, collateralised by the NFT. The company has already facilitated thousands of loans. And, unlike your local pawn shop, you don't need to trust the owner.

A final note about NFTs. The Ethereum standard that was proposed and adopted and coded to support NFTs in January 2018 is called ERC-721, as we have seen. Then along came a project called Enjin that proposed and developed a protocol called ERC-1155, which allows the wrangling of both fungible and non-fungible contracts in the same smart contract. It was originally developed to enable NFTs for swords and shields and the other treasures in videogames, as well as videogame coins, like gold ingots, that are designed to be completely fungible within the game.

Fungible and non-fungible tokens in the same smart contract. One wonders where this could lead.

On August 22nd, 2021 Visa very publicly spent $150,000 to purchase a tiny pixelated NFT-enabled CryptoPunk graphic. They were clearly making a statement. Even the biggest of TradFi sees this market coming, and wants to play.

CHAPTER 16

Mutants and strange creatures - WeirdFi

DeFi took root quickly once Ethereum and smart contracts were available. There were certainly wonks and futurists who had predicted that traditional financial services were going to be rebuilt and deployed on these new platforms, but it seems to us that the innovation, in many cases, came from utterly unexpected places. The creative brains behind some of the services now managing billions in value were often very young, far too young to have had anything more than a surface understanding of how banks developed and how they worked behind their secure access-controlled doors. With some exceptions, they only really knew financial institutions from the customer viewpoint, and they figured they could do better.

Among the DeFi innovators there were very few MBAs, and apart from Robert Leshner of Compound (who had studied economics and worked in banking) and Hugh Karp from Nexus Mutual (who came directly from the insurance industry he is helping to change) few had formal institutional experience. Most of the other founders were computer and maths nerds, with a smattering of lawyers, a biochemist, a physicist and others with wondrously diverse backgrounds. What a joyful irony that these people were trying to do battle with industries in which they had little experience. The people *within* those industries, particularly banking, seemed to have little interest in finding uses for the new technology, aside from some attempts to use centralised block-chains internally (also referred to as 'permissioned' blockchains). When major companies like IBM and Microsoft threw their hats into the ring with showy new offerings, financial institutions assumed that these large external IT companies would arrive on their doorsteps with attractive uses and value propositions for their new products which would somehow tool them up for this blockchain future.

But these, and others of the world's biggest tech companies seemed to have utterly misread the market, the use-cases and the technological zeitgeist. They also built infrastructures which completely violated the concept of decentralisation, reducing blockchains to little more than inefficient databases. Few people were interested in using them. When IBM and Microsoft 'quietly' shut down or vastly reduced their blockchain services in 2021, it was damning. It is also surprising that they missed an obvious point: that the whole reason for a blockchain's being is to enable trust in a network where there are no central authorities and third-party intermediaries. If you insert this authority, then all that Proof-of-Work or Proof-of-Stake is for naught.

For the shambolic collection of entrepreneurs with fresh eyes and furious ambition, a couple of decades of experience in the industry they were attacking could only have been a hindrance. They wanted to start from scratch and reinvent things; a long and determined financial career might have blunted them.

Many crypto initiatives have failed, particularly those that sought to offer new cryptocurrencies to the market, essentially grasping onto the coat-tails of Ethereum and Bitcoin and trying to do something similar, but with new clothing. And similarly, many DeFi initiatives have come and gone, victims either of a better mousetrap or of an ill-considered or badly timed financial service that no one had much interest in.

But sprinkled in among the successful DeFi projects mentioned in these pages, there arose a set of services generally referred to as WeirdFi. We note that some of the projects originally lumped into WeirdFi are now large and successful; Yearn was among these early projects widely considered as a little off the beaten track.

We would like to introduce you to just a few of these. Some are artefacts of the technical architecture, others may be gone tomorrow, surely to be replaced by other oddities as the entire DeFi ecosystem stumbles from hype to maturity.

The first WeirdFi story is that of the Flash Loan. First, an appropriately sensationalist definition – in Ethereum and with the collaboration of certain apps, it is possible to loan funds *without* collateral. Free. You don't even get into trouble if you can't pay it back. And that's because it is impossible not to pay it back. Really. Not kidding.

Here's how it works, at least in principle. The entire blockchain architecture requires that transactions are processed in 'blocks' of a finite size. A bunch of transactions are added to the block until it is full, and then the block is processed, one transaction at time, until the block is done and added to the chain that has been built since 2015, in the case of Ethereum. Then the next block is dealt with. For Ethereum it takes about fifteen seconds to process a block. If some nastiness occurs before the block is finished, everything gets rolled back and the block is not added to the chain.

We pause here for a moment. There is no magic in this – indeed, much of computer science offers similar capability. A batch of commands are packaged in a program, which is instructed to do each one sequentially and only signal success when all have completed successfully. Otherwise signal failure and roll back.

So here is what happens.

Some DeFi projects like dYdX and Aave and others have created a facility in their contracts to allow for flash loans. An investor (or developer) can 'borrow' money, say DAI, from Aave *without* collateral. Then the investor can use that DAI for any purpose that can be performed within that same block time of about fifteen seconds. For instance, swapping it for another cryptocurrency on one exchange and then back to DAI on another exchange to take advantage of an arbitrage opportunity. If this all occurs by the end of the block time, the original amount of DAI is returned to Aave's reserves and the investor pockets the profit when the block is processed. The trick is that the DAI was never really 'loaned' to the investor, they were not free to walk away with the loan indefinitely. They had to act instantaneously in putting it to work before the end of the block, but they can't actually move the loan to their own wallet and head off into the sunset.

We are aware that this is difficult to unravel, even for those who know DeFi. So we have tried to come up with a real-world metaphor.

Alice and Bob and Satoshi and Zaynep are sitting in Scott's kitchen, drinking his fine coffee. Scott is very smart and strict. And this is his house, his rules, which he firmly applies. But he also likes his friends, and doesn't want anyone to be uncomfortable.

Bob says to Alice: 'Got a dollar?'

Alice says: 'Yeah, if you need it.'

Bob turns to Satoshi and says: 'How many yen for a dollar?'

Satoshi says: '110 yen.'

Bob turns to Zaynep, who hasn't been listening because she has been playing with her iPhone, and says: 'If I give you 110 yen, what will you give me in dollars?'

Zaynep says: '$1.03.'

Bob turns to Scott and says: 'This all right with you?'

Scott shrugs: 'Sure. On the count of three, everyone please pull out your money and do the exchanges, FAST!'

And so in a flash (sorry about the pun) Alice gives a dollar to Bob who gives a dollar to Satoshi who gives 110 yen to Bob who gives it to Zaynep, who gives him $1.03. Under Scott's watchful eye.

Bob hands a dollar back to Alice and pockets 3 cents.

Had Zaynep offered 97 US cents for Bob's 110 yen, Bob wouldn't have done the trade, not wanting to lose money, and would have handed back the 110 yen to Satoshi who would have given the dollar back to Bob who would have given it back to Alice. Alice was never in danger of losing her dollar in the first place, because it was not unconditionally loaned. But Bob exploited it anyway.

It is sort of hairy, this zero-collateral facility, unique to DeFi and, until recently, only available to developers. Not surprisingly, there has been some abuse, some hacks, some even smarter flash-loaners outwitting other flash-loaners by using techniques called 'front-running' (explained later) and other weapons of financial war.

The cleverest of them are now making a great deal of zero-risk money, which obviously raises the question: Is it fair? DeFi is supposed to be the great leveller, the agent of financial democratisation.

Eventually it will be, we are sure of that, but on the way there will be wormholes in the financial universe which open up and some of the first partygoers will get rich.

The next WeirdFi project is the lottery in which you cannot lose money. There are a few of these, but the one we'll discuss, the largest, is a protocol called PoolTogether. The concept is simple. Punters put their money in one of a number of pools – a DAI pool or a USDT pool – in return for POOL tokens which give them governance rights. PoolTogether then invests the pooled funds in an external interest-bearing DeFi project like Compound. The interest on the pools is then put up as prize money, and released to the lucky token-holders who have been randomly selected by the system. PoolTogether itself is a protocol and not a lottery, so it allows the design of different types of lotteries under its umbrella by external developers. As long as they conform to its rules they can be inventive, like allowing for different sorts of pay-outs and prize strategies. And of course, POOL tokens given to lottery bettors trade freely on various DEXs.

This might seem astonishing at first glance – a lottery where you deposit money, play weekly, never lose your money and are able to withdraw your funds at will. But this sort of thing has equivalents in the non-virtual worlds, first popularised by Premium Bonds which were launched in 1956 to encourage the war-fatigued British public to save by offering weekly cash prizes drawn from the underlying interest. But again, as in much of DeFi, the main difference from real-world equivalents lies in deployment – easy to deposit, easy to withdraw, easy to design your own lottery and to have its innards open for inspection.

At the time of writing, PoolTogether, which launched in 2019, had awarded hundreds of millions and had nearly $200m locked up in its pool. Not pure DeFi, we know, but a gambling/DeFi hybrid, a combination that also has a long and occasionally less than salubrious history in TradFi. On the other hand, PoolTogether can be viewed through a DeFi lens. It is creating a liquidity pool by offering prizes instead of yield. The pool itself is being put to work in the service of other DeFi projects which use the capital for financial services. It is actually doing no more than liquidity mining to people who understand a 'no-lose-lottery' better than they understand yields, staking and liquidity provision.

The other technology where weirdness abounds is NFTs. We already know about startling prices being paid for NFT-certified art of uncertain talent, but the world warps even further when one considers some of the binding of NFTs to real-world objects. NFTs cleave well to digital objects: the creators simply need to make a digital signature of the digital object, a straightforward cryptography operation. But how does one get a digital signature of a physical object?

Consider Berlin-based Look Labs. According to Forbes.com, in mid-2021 Look Labs released a perfume labelled (without any irony, we expect) Cyber Eau de Parfum. The NFT is bound to the company's use of a fancy scientific machine called a spectrograph to record 'molecular vibrations' emanated by its new perfume, along with the associated bottle and label. There is associated hype that some future AI could recreate the perfume from the digital signature of the spectrographic record, a claim probably meant to be taken with a pinch of salt. There are other companies finding sunlight in the new NFT-to-physical-object world. One is DUST Identity in Boston, which uses a patented device that can cover a part of an object with a nano-diamond 'dust' which is non-cloneable and permanent, something to do with the orientation of the diamonds. To which a digital signature can be generated, and so easily attached to an NFT.

In other areas of WeirdFi there's Alchemix, a company that will loan you money and then pay back the loan for you. You never pay it back. Alchemix does. It sounds impossible, but here is how it works. You hand over some DAI to Alchemix. They give you a loan back, some other currency, for you to do with what you want. But they take the original DAI you handed over and invest in high-yield instruments like Yearn. They use that yield to pay off your loan, keeping some for themselves. It seems like a magic trick, but it will work as long as yields remain high, which obviously cannot sustain for ever.

And how about ARCx? This project seeks to give 'reputation points' to users of DeFi. If you never trade, but just use inefficiencies in the confusion of this young industry to make money, you will be penalised by receiving worse financial returns. If you participate in DeFi the way it was intended (we raise an eyebrow here), you get better returns. Hmm. We're not sure about this one.

Finally, a DeFi company called Sablier, not so much weird as unique. They have built a system to enable streaming money, with applications that seem endless. Time slices of the streaming money are flexible, as is the choice of cryptocurrency. As an example, a worker could be paid by the minute, and have her pay deposited as Bitcoin or Ether or Tether, or even interest-bearing tokens, saving the receiver from having to decide what to do with the incoming stream. Micropayments, one of finance's big headaches, are solved with this technique. And of course, a gift of a governance token or two for your loyalty.

This sector is awash with fecund ideas. Strange creatures are emerging all the time, some hacked in a teenager's garage, some bashed together at DeFi hackathons and some carefully planned and developed by crypto veterans in their 30s who have seen it all. We compare this to similar times as the Internet took hold in the 1990s and smartphones took hold in the noughties. Those days also saw the emergence of strange creatures, but somehow they seemed tamer than this. Most of those were about getting users to eventually buy stuff that was advertised through digital channels, or to subscribe for content, and still are.

But DeFi is closer to the core of things – it is about the very act of value creation, the fire at the centre of human exchange. There is enough energy here for all manner of creatures, and some will be weird enough to gain attention, some will be weird enough to be extinguished with prejudice.

CHAPTER 17
Risks aplenty

The World Economic Forum, with its headline-grabbing annual meeting in Davos, is about as sober an institution as one can imagine. One thousand of the world's largest companies are members, and those few days at the end of each January are packed with not only suited CEOs, but entertainment celebrities and the top rung of politicians. Matters of great import are discussed at length, covering advanced technology, global public–private cooperation and security, and for the remainder of the year various papers and articles are produced, many of them finding their way into research that will eventually influence national and global economic affairs.

So it was with some surprise that a white paper from WEF landed on our desk in June 2021 entitled 'Decentralized Finance (DeFi) Policy-Maker Toolkit'. The organisation regularly covers advanced technologies, with a stated focus on the oft-abused term 'fourth Industrial Revolution', but the surprise was that they had tackled a new industry so young, still struggling for its own identity, and largely unheard of in the greater world. In this paper, the authors outline their view of the risks in DeFi to propose a regulatory toolkit for those readers who need it. Our reading of the risks is slightly different, but only in nuance, emphasis and taxonomy, not in principle. We will paint our own picture here.

Not only is DeFi brand-new, at least when compared with a modern banking and financial system that has been hundreds of years in the making, but it is also unorganised, largely untested, unregulated and evolving and morphing in ways that hobble, if not defy, future-gazing. Having got its start only a few years ago, DeFi projects have blossomed and then grown promiscuously, some withering away, and multitudes taking their place. Today, DeFi looks nothing like it did a year ago, and the same will be true next year.

This is all to say that the risks inherent in the projects that are surviving and growing and already attracting billions of dollars of customers' funds are not easily measurable. DeFi is an actuary's nightmare. There is little data on which to formulate a risk management strategy.

It is just as true that many of the larger projects are already into second- and third-generation releases, which includes the larger projects we have discussed. Even these 'mature' projects have identified problems including security or systemic or economic vulnerabilities and have subsequently rethought and rewritten and patched them in new versions. But it is early days. The industry is sprinting through rough terrain without a helmet. People are going to get hurt along the way.

This was true of the Ethereum and Bitcoin blockchains too, when they launched. Young, experimental, untested. While Bitcoin's blockchain has never been hacked, its interface to the external world has, numerous times. Exchanges and wallets, mainly, but also via other ingenious exploits, such as malware that replaces wallet addresses from your laptop's operating system 'copy-and-paste buffer'. Ethereum is similar, in that the core blockchain has never been hacked. But Ethereum comes with its Solidity smart contract programming language (and other subsequent languages like Vyper), which in turn has enabled all manner of apps, including all of DeFi. The addition of a programming language opened a Pandora's box of risks, some of which have become borne out by fiery crashes, like The DAO hack described earlier.

Bitcoin developers, referred to as 'core developers' are also notoriously meticulous in vetting new protocols and changes to the codebase. New submissions are vigorously debated, reimagined and deployed to a test blockchain called a 'testnet' for experimentation for long periods before being reconsidered for submission to consensus by the network. The actual monetary policy of Bitcoin, meanwhile, is considered sacrosanct and has remained immutable since the first version as set by Satoshi Nakamoto. Bitcoin is reliable, predictable, slow to change.

Not so in DeFi-land where experimentation happens out in the wild, policies are amended seemingly on the fly, and protocol changes are blasted out at regular intervals.

Not all of the risks are clustered around bad actors trying to steal money, of course, although it should be highlighted that some of the bad guys trying to hack into this river of wealth are among the smartest crooks in the world. Swarms of crypto hackers, technologically sophisticated and rabidly incentivised to drain easy billions, are hard at work, every second, in every country, probing the surfaces of crypto for weak spots. It is rumoured that North Korea is largely funded by cybercrime, but whether it is boring old ransomware or something more sophisticated, no one knows. But you can be sure that they are clustered around DeFi.

And so a war rages on the Ethereum network. On one end are opportunists seeking out contract bugs, liquidation opportunities, and other mechanisms for quickly extracting value with clever code. On the other are 'white hats' seeking out vulnerabilities and proactively contacting the relevant parties, or exploiting the bug themselves, safely taking custody of at-risk tokens until the rightful owners can be contacted and the tokens returned.

One such white hat, who operates under the pseudonym 'samczsun', corralled a group of like-minded hackers in September 2020 to work through the night to rescue about $10 million-worth of Ether from a vulnerable smart contract.

In a blogpost, samczsun writes:

'The contract held over 25,000 Ether, worth over 9,600,000 USD at the time, and would be a very juicy payday for anyone who managed to find a bug in its logic.

'I quickly looked through the code for where Ether is transferred out and found two hits. One of them transferred the Ether to a hardcoded token address, so that could be ignored. The second was a burn function that transferred Ether to the sender. After tracing the usage of this function, I discovered that it would be trivial for anyone to mint tokens to themselves for free, but then burn them in exchange for all of the Ether in the contract. My heart jumped. Suddenly, things had become serious.

'And yet on a late Tuesday night, our unlikely group united under a common cause and worked tirelessly to try to ensure that over 9.6 million dollars would be returned to their rightful owners. All of our efforts over the last 7 hours led to this single pending transaction and the spinning dots that came with it.

'When the loading indicator finally turned into a green checkmark, the tense silence on the call gave way to a collective sigh of relief. We had escaped the dark forest.'

The 'dark forest' metaphor is taken from science fiction author Liu Cixin's *Remembrance of Earth's Past* trilogy in which he imagines a 'social cosmology' in which an intelligent species' best chance for survival in the universe is to remain silent, so as not to attract attention from more powerful players.

When such vulnerabilities are identified, acting on them is a dangerous move, as it exposes the rest of the network to said vulnerability. Samczsun had led his ragtag group of hackers in constructing a robust solution.

But there are other risks too, other potential potholes and broken glass and cliff edges that have nothing to do with crime. We will cover the entire gamut below.

Smart contract bugs

No matter how smart a programmer is, bugs are a constant companion in programming. A necessary companion, some would say, at least during development. They serve to alert the programmer during testing that he or she has forgotten something. Not catered for this or that unexpected input or hardware glitch or left-field condition. And even with exhaustive testing and tools, undiscovered bugs occasionally make it through to a final product. Even the best and most experienced programmers admit this.

And so it is with smart contracts, which is why they are often audited externally, sometimes at great expense, to ensure full bug extermination. Because once they are let loose they cannot be quickly or easily changed. This is one of the reasons why the design of Solidity had the expectation of short contracts. The longer the program, the more chances of bugs.

Bugs are not necessarily catastrophic and are often spotted and found by honest actors, who will alert the contract author, who might choose one of a number of mitigation actions, including a fork (meaning an entirely new contract; one cannot send a patch to a smart contract, as it is locked). But occasionally a bug will be spotted by a bad guy, who might find a way to exploit it to steal tokens.

Has this happened? Yes. The most famous hack mentioned earlier in the book was The DAO hack, early in the evolution of DeFi. Over $150 million was stolen while the founders of Ethereum watched in horror as it happened over a period of days. Because smart contracts are immutable, they could only stand by helplessly, at least at first. They were able to eventually stop it via a fancy counter-attack, causing Ethereum to have to reinvent itself by forking off to a new identity and rule-set, which threatened to kill off the entire project. This story has all the dramatic elements of a Hollywood thriller, beautifully described by Camila Russo in her book *The Infinite Machine*, mentioned earlier.

Of course, a smart contract bug may also trigger other systemic problems unrelated to crime, such as a contract not performing the function it was intended to perform, which could have outsized knock-on effects, like a sudden loss of confidence and fast exit of contract users, potentially causing the collapse of an associated token price.

One of the most famous of these was the collapse of the YAM protocol in August 2020. The DeFi protocol, a stablecoin-underpinned yield return application, had a number of innovations built into it – a unique stablecoin monetary algorithm, a 'fair' distribution of YAM governance tokens to every participant

– meaning no founder shares and a firm 'no' to venture capitalists seeking early low-priced tokens, and a complete on-chain governance regime, whereby all decisions were controlled by an immutable governance contract. The protocol was launched on August 11th, instantly attracting huge interest, and by August 12th had amassed liquidity to nearly $500m. One of the core innovations of the protocol was the slicing off of a portion of yields into a development treasury, to be used to further the protocol per the wishes of the YAM governance community.

Everything was going swimmingly until 6.00pm on August 12th. Money was pouring into the pool, the YAM price was soaring, the stablecoin monetary system was behaving. But the smart contract had never been audited, and it had apparently been written in a little less than two weeks. That is asking for trouble. And, almost inevitably, a bug surfaced in the execution of the 'rebase', where yield capital was allocated from the pool to the development treasury. Which caused the governance voting mechanism embedded in the smart contract to fail. Meaning there was no one governing the system, and most importantly it could not be changed, because smart contracts cannot be edited, as we have seen. The story gets a little deeper. A governance work-around was indeed attempted, but then a second bug popped up – the work-around could not be executed by the solidly recalcitrant contract. And so everything went south. About 75% of the staking participants got their funds out. But the YAM token price went from a high of $160 to less than $1 in a day. By 8.00am on the 13th it was all over. It had lasted about three days.

Brock Elmore, its creator, tweeted: 'i'm sorry everyone. i've failed. thank you for the insane support today. i'm sick with grief.'

Yes, we imagine so.

The overriding risk is not that smart contracts may contain bugs. It is that these bugs, whether they are exploited by bad actors or simply destroy contract confidence, are likely to cause massive loss, far more so than a mugging at an ATM or a crooked accountant in a bank back-office or a miscalculated entry on a company balance sheet.

This issue suddenly became front-page global news in August 2021, when a project called Poly (which was mainly used in China; it is a technology to link different blockchains) was drained of the extraordinary sum of $681 million, in various cryptocurrencies. The story moved quickly. After the initial shock, which reverberated well beyond the crypto community and into the nightly news and social networks of the world, a further rumour indicated that a Chinese cybersecurity company, SlowMist, had managed to track down the hackers' identity (with the implied threat of a long prison sentence). Within a few hours Poly had been contacted by the hackers, claiming they were white hats and were planning to return the money.

The money started flowing back to Poly, then slowed down; the hackers and Poly negotiated for a bounty reward, and it was fully returned within a few weeks. While the details of intent and motive are still a little opaque, what is certain is that, firstly, hackers can easily switch hats, and secondly, the potential magnitude of a successful heist is eye-watering (which will surely attract more and more smart bad guys looking for a historic score). In one of the mails to Poly, the hackers write: 'We are going to be legends.' They got that right.

Everyone is scared of smart contract bugs. An entire third-party certification industry has sprung up, offering audits of code, using the finest minds and the smartest tools. And so has a contract insurance industry, offering risk cover in exchange for premiums, as we saw in the chapter on Nexus Mutual. It is telling that the traditional insurance companies could only stand and watch uncomprehendingly as new DeFi insurance projects emerged to offer coverage to users of smart contracts. It is a new expression of an insurance product because it is encapsulated in … smart contracts. Running on the Ethereum blockchain, just like the contracts they are insuring.

Composability risk

Earlier we introduced the term 'money lego', referring to a single financial smart contract available for use by anyone. A nice visual emerges. All of these little smart contracts (they must be green, right?), each providing an atomic and self-contained financial function interacting with other legos, building on each other to provide a much more complex financial service, facilitating a near-infinite variety of services. This concept, incidentally, has long existed in traditional computer programming, via 'micro-services', communicating through standardised gateways called Application Programming Interfaces or APIs.

But this is slightly different, because Solidity and other smart contract languages are not 'general-purpose' languages; the smart contracts are designed for wrangling financial tasks, like transferring value from address to address. The ability to plug these money legos into each other is called *composability*. A financial designer can compose a solution by merely building up from lego blocks. It is efficient, quick and easy for even a single developer to construct a complex financial offering.

Here is an example from the site https://our.status.im/. Ignore the actual DeFi projects or crypto tokens mentioned – this is just a taste of the sort of money lego modelling that is done.

1   Take out a loan of DAI on Compound.

2   Split that DAI into two even amounts.

3   Put one half into Oasis and generate 8% interest.

4   Put one half into a leveraged position for ETH on DeFi Zap.

5   Pull out the funds from both at a given price level of ETH.

6   Repay the loan and interest back to Compound.

7   Keep the remaining balance earned from the leveraged position (assuming ETH price went up).

This product can be built and tested and staged for live launch in days, if not hours. How long do you imagine a bank would take to build a new product of this complexity? Months? Years? How many developers would be assigned? And would you, the retail provider of capital, ever be shown the inner workings of such a product? Not a chance.

Composability is clearly powerful, but the risk of smart contract bugs is now exacerbated. Not only does each money lego have to be bug-free, but multiple connected money legos add another layer which needs similar good health. The complexity of the system grows with each new money lego block, and its risk grows non-linearly as the entire solution gets bigger and bigger, relying on more interdependencies.

There is one further wobble which adds to risk. DeFi projects are increasingly using oracles like Chainlink (described in more detail earlier in this book), which are crypto services and contracts providing access to real-world data, like commodity prices or interest rates, sourced from a traditional data feed such as Bloomberg. Which causes, like some science fiction script, a portal to open between DeFi and the real world, with all manner of mischief that can occur, including the possible manipulation of external data before it is seen by the requesting contract. Oracle providers are profoundly aware of this and go to great lengths to verify the data (not unexpectedly, via decentralised, or at least distributed consensus mechanisms), and to have the data agreed as reliable by the contracts which seek to use them. But the borders between the external off-chain world and the DeFi on-chain world require aggressive vigilance.

It is highly likely that occasional small and large horrors indicated by composability risk will come to pass. And as we said, some people will be hurt. Maturity will come later. Justine Humenansky, one the keenest observers on the deep technical/financial implications of DeFi, provides this quotable quote: 'Composability enables rapid innovation, but it also means that money legos can quickly become money dominos.'

Vampiric arbitrage bots

We are not going to get too down and dirty here (because it's really complex), but we love the horror movie name, so it gets a high billing in this chapter. DEXs allow you to swap one token for another. Because there are numerous pools of liquidity spread across numerous projects, malicious code in a DEX ecosystem could surreptitiously seek the best deal, scalp a little off and send it to a 'vampire' wallet before executing your trade, which is not quite as good. This might be outside of the main smart contract (the contract code of course is open and transparent and can be analysed by anyone, so mischief would be quickly spotted) but may be hidden in, say, a web front end that collects the orders. It's all very arcane and deep in the technical weeds, and at least one such DEX has been accused of doing this. It also needs to be noted that arbitrage bots and what is called 'front-running' (the ability to find out someone's price offer before it is filled and jump ahead of them in the transaction queue to get an unfair edge) is practised regularly in TradFi, and because the perpetrators (usually large investment banks) do not lift their skirts, it has been done with impunity for decades. It is not criminal activity in TradFi and nor are these bots criminal in DeFi. Just perhaps a little prejudicial to the normal trader, and an area of opportunity for some libertarian coder to stamp out the practice.

Systemic risks

When we talk about systemic risks, we are referring to the risks of the entire DeFi and cryptocurrency space. The volatility of the price of many of these tokens is the stuff of crypto lore, with even the staid old-timers like Bitcoin being subject to occasional swings of 5% in a given day, and more. The many smaller tokens, those deployed in the service of the DeFi ecosystem, are even more vulnerable to the sudden roller-coaster, whether caused by sentiment changes or something more fundamental.

Taken by itself, a falling or rising cryptocurrency price, no matter how rapid, should be of little concern to anyone other than its holders, but given the interconnectedness of many DeFi projects, a rapid movement in price can trigger sudden liquidation and frightening contagion, causing a chain reaction that might have serious and unintended consequences far from the original spark.

In the TradFi world we have seen this many times, most recently in the subprime crisis of 2008 and beyond, the damages of which crossed industry boundaries and shuttered many businesses from small to grand, ruined livelihoods on multiple continents and destroyed trillions of dollars of global wealth. Better Markets, a Washington-based research firm, estimated in 2015 that the subprime crisis and its falling dominos will end up costing the world $20 trillion, a number difficult to understand and digest.

There is little that can be done to mitigate this risk in DeFi. The sudden arrival of this new and brash creature from the world of mathematical cryptography has people skittish, even those who are believers. Only 100 million of the global population have put their toes in the water, and some withdraw at the first sign of trouble. It does not help to argue how safe and transparent DeFi contracts are. Users are still risk-averse, and as in old traditional markets, fear still rules.

DeFi designers may try to build robust defences against systemic shocks like sudden price swings, but they will still happen. This being said, a terrifying 50% crash in the price of crypto-assets over a few weeks in June 2021 did not result in systemic collapse – the ecosystem's first major shock showed surprising resilience, no dominos fell, and exchanges and liquidity pools continued to do their work.

Memetic mischief

One of the most written about financial events of 2021 was around the community of retail traders who gathered on a Reddit forum called WallStreetBets. A large number of these traders, acting in concert and fuelled by memes and politics, caused a spectacular rise in price of various assets, including GameStop and others. The details of how this happened are legend, but what was important was that the word spread quickly and powerfully through Reddit and other social channels, memetically. This drove the price of one of the assets, GameStop, from a pallid $20 in early January to a high of nearly $400 a few weeks later.

A similar aberration was seen in the exponential rise of the price of Dogecoin, a Bitcoin-like cryptocurrency that was essentially copied from open source and launched as a sort of crypto in-joke by software engineers Billy Markus and Jackson Palmer. Palmer apparently has not made any money from it, but that could also be an in-joke. A single tweet from Elon Musk fuelled and ignited the Dogecoin rocket. Dogecoin was essentially an also-ran in the crypto world, close to dormant. It rose to become the fifth-biggest crypto asset by market capitalisation in a little less than four months, with a dizzying rise of 70-fold to $70bn at its peak. These price rises were driven by tens of thousands of very small trades, not hundreds of big ones; small traders can move prices as easily as large ones. Not only did Elon Musk drive a sharp rise in Dogecoin, he has been able to wipe tens of billions off the value of Bitcoin with a few sharp Twitter barbs.

Whether or not the rise in prices of these assets will be sustained is not the point. It is rather that the Internet has enabled memes (and misinformation) to be created and spread with a speed and influence that was not possible before, and particularly before the rise and reach of social media. And memetic behaviour has power, sometimes entering the cultural DNA of millions, and driving real-world behaviour.

This risk will spill over into DeFi. Rumour and obfuscation and cynical pump-and-dump narratives have been a feature of the crypto landscape since its birth. It is a risk to the future of DeFi, and one that is hard to quantify.

Regulation

The subject of regulation of cryptocurrency in general (and DeFi in particular) has caused much consternation among policy-makers worldwide, in every country where citizens and companies have turned their eyes and money towards what they see as a possible better alternative to handle the custody and transfer of digital assets. Central bankers and their government overlords have looked in alarm as trillions of dollars have drained out of the traditional finance world and into this strange new world, sometimes hidden from view, as covered in this book.

Before the end of the last decade the amount of money in cryptocurrency and blockchain financial services was merely curious when it was a few tens of billions of dollars. There are now trillions invested, and that is a whole different matter for regulators.

Consequently, we have seen ham-fisted or ill-informed or knee-jerk reactions by regulators, from outright bannings to injunctions, retractions, guidance, laws, repeals, about-turns and general confusion everywhere from China to India to the US. In short, nobody knows what the hell to do, or if anything should be done at all. And nobody seems to agree with anyone else, from Switzerland's Zug canton which has said, 'Come here, you are welcome', to Iran, which has wagged ominous fingers at everybody, to Turkey which has banned Bitcoin outright, to the quiet state of Wyoming which is at the cutting edge of crypto regulation. Not to mention one arm of governments making crypto policy announcements that are contradicted by another, as has happened multiple times in China.

The most direct and successful attempts at tax regulations in this new world were originally at the point where cryptocurrencies are returned to fiat currency at a traditional financial institution. Meaning when a funds transfer is made from a crypto exchange to a bank or vice versa. Governments can see this border crossing and impose their will. Some countries like the US are not even waiting for return to fiat, demanding taxation of profits from every crypto trade, even when it is never taken back to a traditional financial institution.

Taking a look at tax laws around the world is a bewilderment. In Israel, crypto is taxed as an asset. In Bulgaria as a financial asset. In Switzerland as a foreign currency. In Argentina and Spain crypto profits are subject to income tax. In Denmark profits are subject to income tax but losses are deductible. And in the UK corporations, unincorporated businesses and individuals are all taxed differently.

There are also financial and monetary regulations, policies and laws well beyond tax matters, libraries of them. But those are also fraught. For instance, arguments continue about what crypto tokens actually are. Currency? Commodity? Property? Shares? Not all regulators agree, and not all countries agree.

There is, in short, global crypto-regulatory chaos.

This is a large debate, unprecedented. It is not clear when or how or if future regulations will land, and with what force and with what global authority. Regulations surrounding financial and monetary affairs are endless – they seek to protect consumers, to maintain monetary and fiscal stability, to give the economy the best chance to grow, to extract fair tax. They insure, protect, cocoon, oversee, and police.

But there is a problem with some of their application to crypto-currencies in general and DeFi in particular, both of which started off life entirely unregulated, and for which many participants would prefer that it remain that way. Many of these traditional financial regulations and laws were written for an industry that looked nothing like crypto, and are either inappropriate or difficult to enforce. Putting a pin in this, on August 5th, 2021, Gary Gensler, Chair of the US Securities and Exchange Commission, tweeted: 'Rules mostly adopted 16 yrs ago don't fully reflect today's technology. We need to look at ways to freshen up our rules to ensure our equity markets reflect our mission: maintain fair, orderly, & efficient markets, and ensure we protect investors & facilitate capital formation.'

But it is just as true that many participants in crypto might actually like to have regulated protection. There are those who believe that tax matters should be honestly executed and wish to do their duty as a matter of good citizenship. And there are those participants who believe that the national authorities should have financial line of sight to transactions to better govern the country. Of course, there are also many who balk against the spectre of this oversight, particularly among the original libertarian pioneers of the field, who imagined a parallel state-free monetary system.

One of the first shots across this bow was heard in the US in August 2021, when three paragraphs were inserted into a Senate infrastructure bill, seeking to extract tax from the crypto industry to help pay for the cost of the implementation of the bill. The language of those three paragraphs was problematic from the outset, displaying a deep lack of understanding of the inner workings of crypto. Various senators proposed more appropriate language, backed by a rising tide of outrage from 50 million US cryptoholders. The details of the unworkable language are less important than this – if you have read this far, you will agree that this world is novel, complex, bewildering, constantly evolving, and technologically abstruse. There may be some people who understand it in depth, but they are likely not working for the Senate. And it showed.

The hastily edited language changes passed unhappily into law, although the debate around it is still vicious. Then within weeks of this event, both US national and state regulators had let slip the dogs of war, with various actions against DeFi activities of companies like Coinbase, BlockFi and Celsius. And with more to come, warns SEC Chairman Gary Gensler. So the regulation story does not yet have an ending, or even a predictable direction, and more confoundingly is unfolding differently in different jurisdictions globally, none of which has oversight of an industry that lives in a global decentralised cloud. But given what is at stake, we suspect that these are mere skirmishes before mighty and ugly hostilities erupt between the innovators and regulators and financial giants whose territory is under threat.

It is also not clear whether some projects and people who object to the intrusion of the state will retreat further into the anonymity afforded by the maths in order to sidestep regulation, or perhaps for darker reasons. Or, on the other hand, at least on the matter of taxation, maybe to step forward to say: 'Here, this is what I have and what I have been doing, I have nothing to hide, how much do I owe?' Perhaps one can surmise that dishonesty is as equally and minimally distributed in TradFi as it is in crypto.

And then there is the issue of time-frame. Laws and regulations come about slowly in any country you care to name. White papers, green papers, public comment, committees, promulgations, contestation, redrafts. Regulation operates in the time-frame of years, while financial innovation will just blaze forward regardless in the time-frame of the Internet. Policy and regulation will struggle to keep up. The implications of this are entirely opaque. But governments and regulators carry big sticks which can be used against DeFi, perhaps blunt, misdirected and ill-informed. DeFi innovation is moving so fast that it cannot even be described properly, let alone measured; how do you regulate that?

Can this entire industry be brought to a screeching halt by the heavy boot of ill-fitting regulation? We would argue not. On one side a bunch of smart, young and wily innovators building a better and safer and fairer financial system than has existed for millennia.

On the other side, banks and governments seeking to maintain control. We would bet on the innovators.

And so we are shortly to meet one Caitlin Long, in our next chapter, who will take us by the hand and walk us through the no-man's-land between these two armies, and we will find out what she has done to start clearing a path to order, almost single-handed.

Technology risks

There are a number of risks that fall into a broader category of technology design, which will eventually be solved, because they are essentially engineering problems, and engineering problems are often solvable by better engineering. They are:

- High fees resulting from network overload, covered earlier in our discussion of the Trilemma Dilemma.
- Private key protection (lots of ongoing effort here by hundreds of companies; biometric keys are likely to eventually triumph – iris and voice and face recognition and the like).
- Ease-of-use (this is a design problem; projects will solve this or lose users).
- Interface malware at the point at which humans touch block-chain systems, like crypto wallets, which have had multiple failures.
- Threats from quantum computing overcoming key encryption algorithms.
- Miners using flash techniques (remember flash loans?), front-running transactions to gain small arbitrage advantages (not so much a risk, but an actuality, happening daily).

Risks all, but transitory. Most of these applied to the development of the Internet too, and were solved.

Long-tail risks

There are four more uncorrelated risks worth mentioning.

The first is long-tail risk – what happens if someone builds another blockchain (combined with a robust contract language) that is better than Ethereum? We have seen previously that it has already been done. Competitors to Ethereum include Polkadot, Solana, Cardano, BSC and others. They would certainly argue that they have a better mousetrap. But like much else in life, the first to grab the land is hardest to dislodge. There is a massive industry around Ethereum – users, developers, projects and support from around the world. We do not believe that this risk is high, and in any case, DeFi would not die in the unlikely event that Ethereum is supplanted. It would simply migrate to the better mousetrap. It is not always the best technology that wins, but the best story. And right now, Ethereum has the best story.

The second long-tail risk is what is called a governance attack. Some of the DeFi projects have awarded or distributed tokens to users that give holders the right to vote on the direction of the underlying protocol, meaning, in some cases like Yearn, that the project is completely distributed and democratised. It is, in principle, possible for a majority of token-holders to band together to take some misdirected or malicious action, morphing the original DeFi project into something unrecognisable and perhaps dangerous. But like much else in this trustless world, the very anonymity of many parties owning governance tokens makes this possibility vanishingly small. Although it would make a fun movie one day for the right crypto-nerd audience.

The third risk is the 'rug-pull', of which there are two types. The first is a 'hard' rug-pull, when the developers of a project, who are very often anonymous, attract capital into the project via incentives of some kind, and then simply abscond. The second, a 'soft' rug-pull, is when the developers simply abandon the project, leaving it unattended. In June 2021 this is what happened to a project called Ponywhale – the anonymous developers simply walked away. Both types of rug-pulls have bedevilled the business, leaving capital providers high and dry. We suppose the moral of the story is: know who the founders are – anonymity breeds temptation.

The fourth, seldom mentioned, risk is the 'developer incentive misalignment' risk. Developers are often awarded free tokens in a project to contribute to development in lieu of salary and before launch. When tokens are eventually released to the public, those in the hands of developers can be valuable, and sometimes life-changingly valuable. If the developers' code has bugs, only discovered later, those developers may be long gone, their tokens long sold. In other words, developers have short-term incentives, but the work they do has to last for much longer. The 'devs' do not have to ride on the train they built. Which increases the risk of buggy code.

Financial risks

There are numerous risks which fall broadly into the category of 'financial', but they are, in some cases, blurred with those already discussed. Any of the previous risks, when actualised, will have financial impact. There are risks like counterparty risks (in which one party in a transaction cannot deliver their end) but given the instant settlement nature of the liquidity pools and AMMs in DeFi, we believe that these will turn out to be manageable.

There has been some concern about collateralisation levels for those taking out crypto loans. What if it is not enough? The crypto markets are known for swinging wildly, and what if there is such a rapid movement that collateralisation ratios are insufficient and parties cannot be liquidated? We point again to the near 50% crash of June 2021. The centre held.

Then there is the 'asset custody' risk. In crypto, the asset itself is interchangeable with the private key. If you have the key, you have access to the asset. Most people do not want the hassle of remembering to store their own keys, and large institutions are increasingly offering this as a service. But custody standards have not yet settled, and there are numerous competing technologies and processes, some of them entirely digital and some of them at least partly digital (like keys printed on metal in underground vaults). This remains an area of risk until third-party custody is both more standardised and tamper-proof.

And, finally, the risk of providing an attractive home for money launderers. But that is not specific to DeFi and has been a niggling bedfellow of cryptocurrencies since the start of the industry. It has become harder and harder to do, though, as blockchain analytics fall under the increasingly high-resolution microscopes of federal and national authorities, in association with companies like Chainalysis. This company releases an annual cybercrime report, its most recent 2021 research estimating that around 2% of crypto transactions support crime. In the non-crypto world that figure is estimated by the UN to be as high as 5% of global GDP. This is hardly an urgent new crisis, notwithstanding the klaxons of alarm from legislators.

Much like in the analogue world, one can expect smarter cybercriminals finding new ways to evade the law, and smarter cops using ever more sophisticated detection tools to solve the crime. Such as it has always been.

The following quote is taken from the World Economic Forum white paper mentioned at the beginning of the chapter: 'DeFi's novelty, as well as the ease of transferring funds and creating complex instruments, may increase the possibility of abuses, whether by the creators of DeFi protocols, the operators of exchanges or third-party manipulators.'

True, but difficult to measure and mitigate.

Conclusion

It is fair to say that the risk-drenched landscape is part of what makes this an exciting time. What will emerge after pain has been taken, after some unfortunates have lost their funds (which has already happened, across multiple projects, for many reasons), and after some projects have crashed to the ground under the weight of inflated expectations or poor performance – after all of that, there will emerge DeFi services with tempered value and hardened digital armour. Many of these services can be safely ignored by the financial industry as 'risky plays', recommending that their customers stay away from them. They will be considered by the old guard as talented and noisy children engaging in crazy behaviour, jumping off swings and eating grubs. But the children are growing up.

CHAPTER 18
Into the thicket – Wyoming

Caitlin Long smiles a lot. Her YouTube interviews make one think that she would be a fine friend. Enthusiastic, smiley, direct, talkative. Breathtakingly well informed on arcane matters of law and crypto and financial regulations. And horses, she knows a lot about horses. You get the feeling that she would give equal effort to successfully planning a kid's party, running a company, or running a government. The list of what she knows about is actually a lot longer, courtesy of Harvard Law School and the Harvard Kennedy School of Government as well as over two decades at a slew of Wall Street power companies like Salomon Brothers, Credit Suisse and Morgan Stanley, as well as the enterprise blockchain company Symbiont. She is also a native of Wyoming, the most underpopulated state in the US, where she now lives. Hence horses. Wyoming is known for national parks and hot springs, but definitely not as a hotbed of advanced financial technology. Interviewers like to ask Long about Wyoming, and why she came back there, after being at the top rungs of East Coast financial powerhouses for decades. She brushes the question off good-naturedly. Family, roots. She has always had one foot in Wyoming.

And then there was crypto.

Long was at Morgan Stanley in the early 2010s when she first noticed Bitcoin, dismissing it quickly as a no-hoper, likely an attempt by naive programmers to overturn long established and deeply embedded norms. But it didn't go away and her interest grew as she started to realise some of the profound weaknesses in the TradFi system which might be addressed by blockchain technologies. Then one day somewhere around 2013 she popped in to talk to Morgan Stanley's CTO at the time, Bryan Bishop. What do you think of Bitcoin, she asked him. It turns out that he has the extremely rare distinction of having been on Satoshi's original email distribution list so was a fount of information and enthusiasm. Long started going to after-hours Bitcoin meets and drop-ins, 'keeping my head down so I didn't get fired', she relates. A senior Wall Street exec at Bitcoin meet-ups in 2014 was a Salem-level blasphemy.

Long's multi-decade immersion in both the high- and low-level details of regulation of finance in the US was extensive. She quickly saw what might be the future of the nascent technology. She zeroes in on it, even now: 'The incumbents [banks] may throw sand in the wheels and the regulators may slow things, but it is simply a better financial technology because it provides real-time gross settlement without intermediaries, whereas the fiat system can only provide delayed net settlement with the assistance of many intermediaries.' What this meant, in practice, was that a blockchain system, in settling in real time, versus a creaky old national clearing and settlement system, had the potential of increasing the velocity of money by up to 100 times. Money would just flow through the system that much faster. Leverage, that inflammable package of fractional lending, was used in TradFi to do this, and it was dangerous. A real-time settlement system would reduce the need for leverage, increase economic activity and vastly reduce instability in the system.

As a banker/regulation expert this was the ticket. Bitcoin meant other things to other people, like personal freedom from oversight or simply a way to speculate. But Long knew from experience that any new financial system needed a bridge to the old, and would have to play nice with both individuals and institutions. TradFi was not going to lie down and submit. Bridges had to be built if crypto was to grow up. Slowly, carefully and with all the forethought that regulators and financial institutions expect.

She had identified what she saw as the big opportunity to improve finance – real-time gross settlement via the blockchain ecosystem. But she also saw other problems that needed solving, and the first of those was custody – ownership and guardianship of the cryptocurrency asset – a surprisingly arcane and legally fraught matter. The second was to get a regulatory body to write legislation to accommodate this new thing. And so she formulated a plan. Perhaps it was a little hazy at first, but not any more.

Stories like these need inciting incidents to fuel the narrative, even serendipitous ones. Long, who had been accumulating Bitcoin for a few years prior to the bull market of 2017, presumably had some discretionary capital available, and had decided to put some of it to altruistic use by endowing a scholarship for female engineers at her alma mater, the University of Wyoming, around the time of the bull market. But she quickly found out that Wyoming could not accept her Bitcoin, due to a confusing and ill-defined legal framework around money transmission. Long had worked in the Wyoming legislature as an intern, and understood a little about the legislative process, so she made some calls and volunteered to help fix the law. One thing led to another, and she settled down in a hotel room in the capital Cheyenne to help fix the money transmitter laws. Which meant speaking to regulators. And reading bills, laws, regulations and policies. And writing stuff down. And drafting positions. And speaking to lawyers and politicians. And technologists. And thinking. And articulating arguments. You know, just the standard stuff competent people do.

Her work ended up fixing the money transmitter regulations. And, it seems, she had made some friends in high places along the way, at least in Wyoming. What else can we do?, they asked. Surely you don't want to go back to New York? Better horses here. Better parks. What can we give you to play with that will keep you here? Any ideas?

Well, yes. She had some.

Let's build a regulatory regime for crypto that will be the most advanced in the country, if not the world. Let's build a set of foundations that will allow crypto banks to operate with confidence in the light of day. Let's bring incumbents and other stakeholders into the conversation. Let's not be adversarial and shrieky. She got the go-ahead from the regulators, and so the Wyoming Blockchain Task Force was born.

Within two years the Wyoming legislature had passed thirteen laws related to crypto, a blazing speed in the regulation game. These started with defining exactly what a crypto asset was. This was essentially a blank canvas – there was little in the way of precedent, but given the state's and Long's passion for property rights, it was no surprise that ownership rights and protections were baked into the definition of a crypto asset. They went much further than that, though, devising mechanisms to define custody and to authorise custodianship by banks, and the protection of crypto-software engineers from lawsuits related to subsequent mal-feasance (by defining computer code as free speech!); they also brought cryptocurrency in line with other commercial monetary regulations, defined the difference (or similarity, as it turns out) between a crypto asset and a private key, and defined under what condition a judge could compel release of a private key. They also exempted crypto–crypto exchange from money transmission laws, banishing uncertainty from peer-to-peer trading, and created a 'fintech sandbox' law to allow innovators to experiment for three years without running afoul of any crypto law.

Probably the most important law was the creation of a charter for a special class of bank, called a 'speedy' or 'SPDI' – Special Purpose Depository Institution. These are non-lending institu-tions, authorised to take deposits from crypto-related institutions like crypto-exchanges, removing a huge thorn from the industry's side, where companies and individuals doing any sort of business with crypto institutions have suddenly found themselves with their bank account brutally shut down as traditional banks exercised caution in an unregulated environment. The SPDIs were required to have 100% capital reserves and so were able to avoid the hurdle of obtaining Federal Deposit Insurance Corporation (FDIC) insur-ance, which would be somewhat redundant without the risks of lending.

The legal framework created by this set of laws was broad and unprecedented. Above all, an environment of legal certainty was created, which released a flood of commercial activity, including big crypto companies like Kraken and Ripple and Solana, all of which have moved their headquarters to Wyoming. Not to mention creating a roadmap for the judges to rule, which had been absent before this.

In reading the commentary around Wyoming's spurt into crypto-regulatory leadership and Long's effusive and voluminous commentaries on social media, it becomes clear to us which of these little revolutions she is most proud of, besides the fact that she sort of led and helped build an entirely new legal framework. This was the issue of a private key owner's *direct* ownership of the digital asset. This might seem tautological ('Your keys, your coins') but it is not. Unbeknown to most people in the US (and perhaps in other national jurisdictions), if you buy a security all you are buying is an IOU from the broker, who has in turn, bought an IOU from the issuer. This is also true, shockingly, of cash. Your dollar is simply an IOU from the central bank. This means, under nasty conditions (bankruptcies, for instance) you may lose access to that which you thought you owned. The legalese around this is a little opaque, with scary words like *bailment* thrown around, but in the case of Wyoming, if you own a digital asset, you directly and actually own it. It is your property, a very precious subject in the history of Wyoming ranching; you do not want to mess with them on this subject. It is indeed pretty revolutionary, especially if you realise that no one in the US directly owns a security they purchased on an exchange, and a judge can award that security to someone else.

Caitlin Long has, unsurprisingly, started a SPDI – Avanti Bank. And she continues to be active in both regulation and the enthusiastic exporting of the Wyoming model to other states, Nebraska being close behind. Of course, US states, while having significant financial powers of their own to wield, still have over-seers, and in order for crypto and DeFi service to spread nationally and globally, many other larger bodies will have to build similar crypto frameworks.

For instance, in the US there are three uber-masters of financial regulation: the Federal Reserve, the Office of the Comptroller of the Currency (OCC) and the FDIC. They usually work in concert, consulting each other on whatever arcana regulators consult each other on. But in the second quarter of 2021, the OCC wrote an 'interpretation' that seemed to indicate that it was fine for traditional banks to deal with crypto companies, which got everyone all excited. Only to be followed up by letters sent by the Fed and other agencies querying which companies were on the do-business-with list. Bank of America got one, for instance. This kind of query is not evidence of wrong-doing, but possibly a precursor to finger-wagging and demerits or lowering of creditworthiness scores. So the banks got all nervous again.

And this is only three agencies from among scores of others at both national and state levels. We have used the Wyoming story to illustrate a larger unfolding of the regulatory complexity. All countries have bodies that are involved in regulation. The UK has the Financial Conduct Authority, the Prudential Regulation Authority and the Financial Policy Committee. To say nothing of multiple tax bodies. The EU has the European System of Financial Supervision (ESFS) comprising the ESRB, ESA, EBA, ESMA, EIOPA. Don't even ask. To coordinate and concretise the regulation of an entire parallel monetary and financial services system is going to be, to put it mildly, a challenge.

The major Bitcoin conference of 2021, uncreatively called Bitcoin 2021, was held in Miami. On June 5th, at a breathlessly anticipated presentation, Jack Mallers, CEO of remittance company Strike, announced that El Salvador had decided to present a bill to parliament to make Bitcoin legal tender in the country. A video was then played, timed in perfect Hollywood fashion – it was the president of the state of El Salvador, Nayib Bukele, announcing that he would propose a new currency law making Bitcoin an equal partner to the dollar. 'Next week I will send to Congress a bill that will make bitcoin a legal currency,' Bukele said. It was passed into law the following week.

Mallers, still in his twenties at the time of writing, had been in El Salvador as a private entrepreneur to enable low-cost remittances between two million expats and Salvadoran citizens, much of the remittances coming from the US. Over 80% of El Salvadorans are not formally banked – remittance from expats is a major source of inbound revenue to this small country of six million. Remittances had been expensive, with as much as 50% being drained away via fees and other overheads. Mallers was having success bringing on board thousands of citizens with a Bitcoin remittance system, essentially free of transaction charges.

News of this got to the president. He invited Mallers over for a chat ('I nearly pissed myself', the young CEO said later). And then, a few months later, the announcement.

People inside the crypto industry cheered wildly – a whole country had just been signed up to Bitcoin. Most other people shrugged: a tiny poor country, who cares? But Caitlin Long saw this differently. To this conservative and sober practitioner of finance and regulation it was a huge deal. In a tweetstorm not more than a few hours after the announcement she said the following:

'What's the big deal – what's "legal tender" anyway? It's a commercial law term (means citizens must accept "X" if offered in payment of an obligation in exchange for delivering property). Legal tender is key to commercial law, which is THE foundational layer of any legal system'

'If #ElSalvador does pass legislation to recognize #bitcoin as legal tender, #BTC would v likely become MONEY under US commercial law (https://law.cornell.edu/ucc/1/1-201: "Money means a medium of exchange currently authorized or adopted by a domestic or foreign govt")'

'... & thereby open the door to treatment of #bitcoin as "money" under commercial law + "cash" under acctg rules.'

'What's the significance? Well, it means #bitcoin would gain special status in banking systems globally. Banks would likely treat it as any other foreign currency. #Bitcoin MAY get back-door favorable treatment under bank capital requirements (Basel 3, etc.).'

Some of this is a little incomprehensible, we know, requiring arcane knowledge of laws and policies and accounting and banking. But her excitement was palpable. The tweetstorm went on for days, expanded, was joined by others, and then really blew up after the law was passed. Debate raged, not so much about the significance of the event (everyone thought it was a big deal), but about its portents. Which countries might follow? Would the US retaliate, or rather how soon and in what form would they retaliate? What would the IMF say? Would it eventually end in a financial catastrophe for El Salvador?

On June 9th, a few days later, a US Senate Bank Committee hearing was due to be held in public, via videoconference. Not much will be remembered about the submissions except for Senator Elizabeth Warren, who warned, in lurid tones, that Bitcoin (and by extension ETH and DeFi in general) needed to be strictly confronted and constrained, perhaps even banned completely. It was not a pretty sight, as she warned of terrible things on the horizon – crime, climate catastrophe, global economic instability. Then – a mere 24 hours later – a report was issued from the Basel Committee on Banking Supervision, the world's most powerful banking standards-setter, with recommendations on how to regulate Bitcoin and DeFi (strictly) and stablecoins (less strictly). But strict does not necessarily mean bad, it means that there are risks and this is new, so keep a tight lid on this until risks subside.

And then on June 10th, guidance from the mighty IMF, which said, hmm, yes, banks might be able to play in the crypto world, but only if it is treated as the highest-risk asset. Meaning, every crypto-asset must be fully backed by fiat collateral. Some commentators said – finally, a path to legitimacy. Others said – what a blow to crypto. The Bitcoin price went up that day.

This is the fight which is shaping up. People like Long have carefully inched their way forward, and been able to lay down deep tracks in Wyoming at least. But at the national level a whole new war opens up, which is likely true in Europe and other countries as well. At stake is no less than who controls global supply, how it is monitored and who has the right to do that monitoring, and what may be done with the information collected. The US probably has the most to lose here – the dollar is the world's global reserve currency, even as America weakens in global influence on many fronts. It is not likely to concede without a metaphorically bloody fight.

But in countries like El Salvador there is a different narrative, for better or for worse. It is built, at least partly, on the need to be free of global dollar dominance and its outsized influence, seen by some to be a proxy for American hegemony. And even for those countries whose initial view of crypto finance may have been one of suspicion and resistance, looking at El Salvador may cause them to say: maybe this is a way for us to break free too. Rumours swirled around at least half a dozen countries, including Argentina, Paraguay, Panama and others, within days of the El Salvador announcement. We expect that by the time this book is on the shelves El Salvador will have plenty of company.

What of Caitlin Long? Building her state-mandated crypto bank Avanti, with a smile.

CHAPTER 19

Fintech - lipstick on a ...

I t is tempting to add the next word, pig, to the chapter title, but that would not be accurate or fair, given the bubbling fintech innovations that have happened over the last ten years. But there is a kernel of truth underneath. Financial technology services are not DeFi, but they are not orthogonal either. They have developed in parallel, also harnessing and exploiting new technologies to slice inefficiencies out of TradFi, and have done so largely by rebuilding customer experiences into something more friendly and efficient than what we have been subjected to for decades by financial institutions. That turns out to be an enormous market. An estimated $140 billion has been invested in fintech over the last decade, and customers have received it with open arms.

But it is not DeFi and has nothing to do with crypto, even though the two are sometimes spoken about in the same breath. What is certain is that fintech will undoubtedly have value to contribute to DeFi, and a merge of skill sets is inevitable.

In search of a definition we turn to Will Beeson. Beeson is a successful serial creator of what are generally called neobanks. These are pretty much traditional banks without retail infrastructure, whose services sit behind modern and sometimes uniquely designed

PC and mobile phone interfaces. Beeson is a CFA (Chartered Financial Accountant) and after starting a traditional banking career at Citi and other TradFi companies, he found himself 'Fed up with the banking industry and trying to do something about it', as is proclaimed proudly at the top of his LinkedIn page. After leaving the corporate world he ended up working as an adviser to various new technologically-led banking ventures, eventually helping to found neobanks Allica in the UK and Bella in the US.

But first – a small matter of nuance. All neobanks fall into the definition of fintech, but not all fintech initiatives are neobanks. PayPal, for instance, one of the most successful fintechs, is not a neobank, it is simply an Internet-friendly front-end for credit card payments. Then there are players like Remitly (remittances), Hudson River Trading (algorithmic trading), Braintree (payment integration), Venmo (peer-to-peer payment), TrueAccord (debt collection), TransferWise (global retail funds transfer), Revolut (cards, global business money transfer and stock trading) – literally hundreds of these 'vertical' fintech companies have chosen deep niches and succeeded, some of them entirely unrelated to banking services. Neobanks sport broader offerings beyond front-ends, some of them providing complete banking services that compete directly with old-school financial institutions.

Beeson had the following to say on The Fintech Blueprint podcast: 'Neobanks create an interesting consumer experience on top of regulated banking infrastructure.' Indeed, that has been the focus of much of fintech – providing consumer experiences that are better than TradFi, and thereby acquiring loyal customers from whom underlying TradFi services are hidden. There is no pejorative implied here, but there is little in fintech that tries to revolutionise the core banking services of TradFi. Of course in the world of DeFi, it is all about *redesigning and replacing* core banking services, not just offering traditional ones behind an improved interface.

In fintech there is also the notion of 'rebundling' financial services as they are unbundled from traditional institutions. For example, London-based Curve (confusingly not the same as the crypto company Curve mentioned earlier) consolidates all of your payment cards into one, offering rewards and other financial services beyond what customers are getting from their other banks and providers. This darling of fintech investors is seen as an exemplar of next-generation financial services, but it does not use cryptocurrency or even blockchain technology anywhere in its stack. Yet.

Beeson describes an interesting dichotomy between the neobanking landscape in the UK/EU (and other countries) and the US. It turns out that the UK and its banking regulator, the Financial Conduct Authority, and the equivalents in the EU, have been aggressive in fostering competition to the traditional 'large' banking sector. They are implementing a consumer-friendly set of laws that has opened cracks in embedded banking interests. This has ranged from Open Banking regulations (which allow third parties to access and offer external services to any bank's customer base) to the fast-track approval of the new, nimble neobanks. In addition to the consumer interaction layer, some of these banks outside of the US have started to compete in core services of borrowing and lending, and have established their infrastructures in the cloud, using modern open-source software stacks, thereby being able to operate more cost-efficiently than the older banks with their large on-premise data centres and layers of technical staff and intermediaries.

In the US, the situation is far more constrained, with protective special interests and complicated state versus federal rights confounding the competitive and regulatory landscape. Neobanks have ended up meaning something different in the US, with new entrants having to be satisfied with simply layering efficient and attractive interfaces on top of, and in collaboration with existing banks' core services.

There is a concept in finance called 'money-in-motion, money-at-rest'. Money-in-motion refers to the movement of money on the back of transactions – payment, spending, transfers – where velocity is king and service providers' business models are fee-based. Money-at-rest describes the more patient business of deposits and long-term investments that one would typically find in a bank, where interest on capital rules the roost, and service providers look to put invested capital to work to return a higher rate than they pay for the original capital investment.

The fintech sector of the last decade has trafficked mainly in money-in-motion, if we ignore the more cerebral new data science and analytics offerings. The reasons for this are obvious. You do not need a banking licence to acquire a customer or to aggregate a transaction, and you can take a small cut as you hand the customer's transaction over to a regulated credit card processor (like PayPal does) or a traditional bank. So most of the original innovation in fintech was around the fee-based money-in-motion. Determined effort was made to create fabulous apps, brimming with intuitive interfaces and youthful design. Using these apps was just, well, more fun than bank-mandated apps using pedestrian front-ends. The designers of these new fintech apps were a different species from bank app designers. They understood customers better, not so much in their financial needs, but in how they like to be talked to. These new app developers understood 'social'; banks seemed to struggle with this. The new entrants also understood principles in design thinking and user experience (UX) development, as pioneered at companies like IDEO and Google – principles which were foreign to the dinosaurs of the banking world until very recently.

This user-focused approach has continued with neobanks, which are simply fintech written more broadly. One of the newer American neobanks, Bella (co-founded by Will Beeson, as we saw) is a perfect example. If you go to the website (the URL being the first clue – www.bellaloves.me), you will be greeted by a video from the CEO. The title under the video reads 'Angelo, our CEO, wants to share with you how BELLA is different'. Angelo. No last name. Just Angelo. On the screen appears this guy. Italian-looking. Tanned, friendly, handsome, sporty face – not too young, not too old. Then he starts talking. Wait! He IS Italian, with a classic accent. An Italian CEO of a US company. What does he talk about? Interest rates? No. Customer service? No. He talks about how pretty Bella's credit card is, and then he kisses it. And then goes on to explain that when you use it you get loyalty rewards which you can use yourself, or pay forward to another Bella user, or donate to a good cause. They call them Karma points. Yes, Karma points. Angelo even uses a bleeped swear word during his monologue.

The difference between this approach and a TradFi bank couldn't be wider. Neobanks are capturing the hearts of their users, even though the neobanks eventually have to hand over their customers' money to a boring old regulated bank sitting in the background in return for a well-earned fee, their reward for displaying customer savvy at the front end. And it goes without saying that the apps themselves are simple and attractive and pleasant to use.

This sort of customer focus is not that evident in DeFi, at least not yet. Although many of the projects in DeFi have gamely tried to build killer user experiences, the results have been spotty. They could do with some help if they want to attract a crowd.

If one takes a look at the roots of fintech and the roots of DeFi, their differences are not hard to understand. DeFi grew almost exclusively out of tech-nerdism. The progenitors were largely people who understood the principles of cryptography and could code, or at least understood the mechanics of doing so. People in DeFi were already interested in money matters, because Bitcoin and Ethereum were monetary systems at their core. So the DeFi pioneers looked to see what the old monetary system offered in the way of core money services, and how that might apply to cryptocurrencies. What they found when they peered into the banks was software systems that were either creaky and designed for another age, or built to accommodate regulations not applicable to cryptocurrencies, or that were not responsive to customers' fondest hopes for fair play, or were simply unable to offer services that could be imagined under a system of interacting smart contracts. So they built their own from scratch.

Fintech and neobank progenitors saw something else. They saw a regulated banking system with fiercely protected core functions which were not likely to change, and banks that had done the boring but critical work of making sure they were in regulatory good grace. So their objective was different. It was – if we are going to have to use this stuff, let's at least make the customer experience as rewarding as possible with all the new technologies that most banks have not had the fleetness-of-foot to absorb.

This was an entirely different objective.

Now, imagine the excellence of fintech's user-experience and marketing savvy applied to the new programmed and interlocking ecosystems coming out of the DeFi world and its redesigned financial service cores.

CHAPTER 20

The great crypto energy debate

Some of us with long memories will remember the time when the Internet was relatively young – the early 2000s. This was when it began to be clear that this new technology had unstoppable commercial and technological momentum and would be used by the majority of the global population at some point in the future.

And some might remember a short, sharp alarm that went off in the popular press, proclaiming that as the Internet spread around the world its energy appetite would break all manner of things, and lead to all sorts of economic troubles. An article from May 31st, 1999 in Forbes.com, entitled 'Dig more coal – the PCs are coming', reported that it takes a 'pound of coal to move 2Mb' and went on to sound energy alarms at klaxon decibels. A report from the Boston Consulting Group as late as 2004 proclaimed grimly that the Internet used 10% of the world's electricity and was responsible for 2% of its carbon emissions, and warned of worse to come. Projections, extrapolations and models were built by smart people; the future of energy usage for a democratised Internet did not bode well, we were told. At best it would be overwhelmingly expensive, at worst it would be a catastrophe for all.

Well, yes. The Internet does indeed use a lot of energy, but not enough to have upended civilisation. Computers, routers, data centres, undersea cables, satellites, radio towers, fibre and ducts and trenching. To say nothing of the energy expended in pushing bits into the pipes – Facebook graduation photos and YouTube cat videos and Netflix movies and the like. In fact, it uses far less energy than was predicted in the 1990s – about 2% of global energy in 2020, according to a report by the US Department of Energy. Thus illustrating the age-old mistake of using simple linear mathematical projections to predict a path that is multivariate and non-linear in myriad ways.

But it is true that this energy was not required before the pre-modern Internet. It was newly produced and/or redirected away from less efficient technologies like the old analogue telephone system and fax machines and printers. No one today, save for the occasional luddite or political malcontent, would argue that the Internet and the energy required to sustain it is a waste of resources. The Internet is useful; we accept that energy usage in the service of utility is a good thing.

But on May 13th, 2021, Elon Musk tweeted: 'Tesla has suspended vehicle purchases using Bitcoin. We are concerned about the rapidly increasing use of fossil fuels for Bitcoin mining, especially coal ...'

Even though there had already been a number of articles expressing concern about crypto-mining and energy usage, Musk's tweet not only helped to catalyse one of the worst crashes in crypto market history, but also pushed the entire issue of energy consumption into the public eye.

It seems we are here again, with a similar debate around the energy usage in crypto as there had been around the Internet. Perhaps nastier this time, with vicious insults hurled back and forth, often obscuring facts in favour of ideology. And not only the Twitter trolls. Academics at storied institutions have bickered, harsh words have been exchanged between normally sober analysts, and news outlets have presented wildly differing reports to the public, presumably depending on the depth (or shallowness) of research or the predilections of any given journalist.

In order to try to understand the nature of this debate, we need to tease apart the interconnected issues. Who is using this energy and how much and where and for what? And is the energy usage worth the benefit gained to society?

Concerns about energy usage have been directed at one pillar in the crypto technology ecosystem. That is mining – which is the incentivised application of compute power to validate transactions and to mint coins as a reward for doing so.

We slow down here to explain mining a little more deeply. Satoshi had to think about how Bitcoins would be 'minted'; how they would get created. Core to this was that it had to be difficult, just as gold has value because it is scarce and difficult (expensive) to mine. His solution to the 'difficulty' question was to make it difficult *computationally* to mint a Bitcoin. The more a computer has to compute, the more energy it needs. So he devised a cryptography problem, a mathematical 'guessing game' which by its nature uses energy, which anyone who wishes to mine needs to solve in order to mint some Bitcoin. This is important – the energy usage in mining is intentional and mimics the real world – if it was too easy, it would have less value. It was even smarter than that: as more miners enter the race to mint Bitcoin, the 'puzzle' automatically gets more difficult, thereby keeping a lid on the minting process.

All miners race to complete the task first (it is the same task for everyone, and the winner is always random). As an incentive, the winner gets some cryptocurrency for their effort. And, through the magic of asymmetric cryptography, all other non-mining transaction validators on the Bitcoin network (called nodes) can check the winning miner's results using very little compute power at all. (Remember from our earlier discussion on this: the algorithm is hard to solve in one direction, but not the other.)

And that is how the transactions are kept honest and that is how the currency is minted. This is all automated. If you want to be a miner, you buy one computer (or many) and download free mining software, plug it in and switch on the power. That's it.

The maths puzzle being computed by the miners in order to mint Bitcoin also has a critical associated function. Various attempts at digital currencies have been proposed and developed for nearly 50 years. There were many problems that made them impractical, but none more than the 'double-spend' problem – how to stop multiple copies of the fungible currency from being copied and spent. Satoshi's solution (which itself was based on previous work by Adam Back, who developed a Bitcoin called Hashcash in the 1990s) was to make the sort of blockchain attack that might enable double spending too expensive to contemplate. In order to carry out that sort of attack, the attacker would have to control a large part of the mining network, and the expense of computation would exceed the rewards.

Mining is supposed to be expensive; it is a security feature, not a design bug.

There are a few matters to be unpacked here, but let's start with DeFi's culpability in energy consumption (as opposed to Bitcoin's).

As discussed, almost all of the major DeFi projects described here run on the Ethereum blockchain; it is the operating system on top of which the entire cornucopia of DeFi innovation rests.

However, as we have seen, Ethereum has migrated *away* from the energy-intensive mining model (called Proof-of-Work) to an energy-light, non-mining model called Proof-of-Stake, due for launch in late 2021 or early 2022.

Upshot? DeFi will not hog energy, not after the move to Proof-of-Stake. DeFi does not rely on Proof-of-Work mining, except for those efforts to carry DeFi projects on the Bitcoin blockchain, of which there are not many. However, we believe that it is worth a short digression into this subject, because, well, energy. Carbon footprint. Climate change. An important topic for everyone.

So which cryptocurrencies use crypto-mining in their process? Bitcoin does. There are others like LiteCoin, but Bitcoin mines dominate. And it is the Bitcoin miners around whom this debate rages. Long before Musk's tweet the matter of energy usage was first raised above the parapet in the magazine *Nature Climate Change* in 2018 by Camilo Mora et al. It came to this startling conclusion: 'Here we show that projected Bitcoin usage, should it follow the rate of adoption of other broadly adopted technologies, could alone produce enough CO_2 emissions to push warming above 2°C within less than three decades.'

The assumptions and techniques in this paper have been shown to be false or misleading or logically fallacious on numerous axes in the years since publication, but once that 2°C cat was out of the bag it very quickly began to meow. Further studies, like those from the Cambridge Centre for Alternative Finance, further entrenched the view that Bitcoin was ravaging the climate and taking energy from more deserving causes. Other memetic alarms took hold. In December 2017, *Newsweek* ran a piece entitled 'Bitcoin Mining on Track to Consume All of the World's Energy by 2020'. Clearly, we are still here. Others trumpeted that Bitcoin energy usage exceeded that of small countries; BBC News in February 2021 claimed that Bitcoin used more energy than Argentina.

It's worth sharing well-known investment strategist Lyn Alden's perspective on this. She writes in a blog on swanbitcoin. com: 'It's easier to sensationalize things for pageviews or political gain. For example, it's commonly said that the Bitcoin network uses more energy than some countries. That's true, but then so does Google, YouTube, Netflix, Facebook, Amazon, the cruise industry, Christmas lights, household drying machines, private jets, the zinc industry, and basically any other sizable platform or industry. From that list, Bitcoin's energy usage is the closest to that of the cruise industry's energy usage, but bitcoins are used by more people, and the network scales far better.'

In any event it turns out that the Cambridge studies and others had made numerous fundamental errors. For instance, the Cambridge study confused the number of transactions with 'hash rate' (compute power and associated energy usage), neglecting the fact that transactions are bundled into 'blocks', which meant that some of their conclusions were an order of magnitude off. Another error was assuming that the miners would use the same mining rig for the next 100 years, a grievously wrong assumption in a world where compute power gets faster and more energy-efficient over time. These studies have also made linear projections about the growth of transactions over time, which are subject to evidence-based contestation. The rate of growth of Bitcoin transactions cannot be extended linearly into the future, because that rate changes over time as new technologies and upgrades and usage patterns are introduced into the system. Innovation constantly rewires projections.

Paul Veradittakit, Investor at Pantera Capital, wrote a well-structured take-down of all the errors in previous research in a

LinkedIn article on his page, published May 13th, 2021, but none is better than the one quoted in his article and attributed to Eric R. Masanet et al. from the Lawrence Berkeley National Laboratory, titled 'Implausible projections overestimate near-term Bitcoin CO_2 emissions', which came about a year after the Mora study and referred directly to it:

> 'The results show that, had the authors avoided the key errors we described above, their own study design would have yielded much different, and far less alarming, projections of future Bitcoin carbon emissions. That said, we find the study design itself sufficiently flawed – e.g., use of transactions as driver, comparisons to 40 unrelated technologies, ignoring rig evolution – that such corrections alone are not enough to salvage the authors' approach. On these bases, we argue that the Mora et al. scenarios are fundamentally flawed and should not be taken seriously by researchers, policymakers, or the public.'

Ouch.

In any event, let's leave these studies behind and try to understand what we know, and don't, about Bitcoin energy usage – and more importantly, what may change in the future.

Because miners tend to be secretive about their operations in order to maintain a competitive edge, there is not much information about what *sort* of power is being used to run the mines, which are often housed in large warehouses with hundreds or thousands of machines. One study from investment company CoinShares estimated renewable power sources to account for 73% of total mining. The Cambridge research reported that 39% of miners used renewables.

Data is thin, and there is certainly a mix, with some renewable and some dirty. But even at the low end of 39% renewable, this is high compared to most countries' internal usage, and twice as high as the energy mix in the US. In any event, all of that changed within a few weeks in May 2021. First came the Musk tweet, which catalysed a later meeting between Musk, the Bitcoin maximalist investor Michael Saylor and a group representing American miners. Promises were made to 'green-up', at least from this group. The second major change-agent around this time was the heavy boot of Chinese law-makers, who kicked the miners out of China, a move we expect that they will come to regret. The miners simply packed their computers in boxes, shipped them to another country, and would have certainly taken note of the green pressure applied at the time they were evicted. The third event, also around the same time, was El Salvador's acceptance of Bitcoin as a digital currency, which was accompanied by an intent to use the massive green power resources available in that small country.

Keep in mind that the overwhelming dominant cost of a crypto-mining operation is the energy cost. The cost of machines and people and rent is very small by comparison. So it is in the service of profit that all miners are constantly in search of the cheapest energy *no matter where in the world it is*. This last part is critical and entirely different from most traditional energy requirements, which need to be near the population centres they serve, or at least near a robust and well-travelled energy grid into which power can be fed. There is no such requirement in crypto-mining. An Internet line and cheap energy is all that is needed. An energy grid is irrelevant.

This has a direct economic consequence for miners. They go where energy is most unused or uncaptured or wasted. Because this is where it is cheapest. This has resulted in a continual decrease in home miners, with most mining being done by professional hubs, far from population centres.

Examples abound. Hydropower, for example. There are hundreds of these plants worldwide and many of them produce more power than can be injected into the grid. A warehouse full of machines located at a power plant is not only going to get very cheap power, it is also not redirecting or taking power away from anybody or anything. It is using stranded energy, otherwise wasted. It is worth belabouring this point. Mining only requires energy, not an electricity grid. This makes it unique among all other electricity consumers.

As another example of this, consider the following quietly growing new business of unlikely bedfellows. Most energy drilling operations are required to burn off excess gas in the field, which is a by-product of their core extraction (mostly in shale operations). You may have seen photos of this – a tall chimney-like structure called a flare stack nearby, spewing flames. This is 'flaring', the burning off of excess gas, being executed under the pressure of regulations, investors and good climate governance. The gas, incidentally, is largely made up of methane, evil stuff, far worse for the environment than carbon.

Somewhere along the line someone looked at this and said – this is wasted energy; surely it can be captured and used to mine Bitcoin? A Russian crypto-miner by the name of Sergii Gerasymovych has been anointed with coming up with this Eureka moment in 2019, as per an article in qz.com. His big idea: instead of burning it away, stick in a gas turbine, generate electricity and send that electricity to a crypto-mine housed in portable containers erected mere metres away. Split the profits between energy company and miner. No energy usage was redirected or stolen from anywhere or anybody else. There is a net benefit of pollution reduction. Everyone wins. Gazprom, Equinor, Wyoming Oil and Gas and a host of other brand names in the oil and gas industry have stepped up, partnering with mining companies with names like EZ Blockchain (Sergii's company), Upstream Data and Crusoe Energy Solutions (Crusoe: *stranded* energy reclaimed. Get it?). Criticisms have been levelled at this particular solution in that it helps the bottom line of old-style oil and gas companies, seen by many as polluters and environmental profiteers. Fair comment, but it is a mere pimple on their balance sheets.

That this example still piggybacks off existing fossil fuel energy production is also fair comment, but it is mitigated by the fact that in this case the mining simply takes advantage of wasted energy by-product, wherever it can find it.

One of the most eloquent spokesmen on the matter of energy and Bitcoin is Nic Carter, who is a general partner at Castle Island Ventures in the US, but more importantly a careful thinker and writer about all things crypto, someone who does the homework. In a 2021 blogpost he coined the term 'nonrival energy'. He defined it as surplus energy which would never have made it to the grid, and which does not deprive anyone else of existing energy. The previously mentioned gas flare capture is a good example.

The Chinese crypto-miners who were shown the door in May 2021 were actually mining in the large under-populated regions of China (Xinjiang, Sichuan, Inner Mongolia, Yunnan) which have a huge oversupply of energy, particularly hydro, and no one to deliver it to. Stranded energy. Nonrival energy, in Nic Carter's phrase. So the reason many miners opened their operations there is that the imbalance of supply and demand drives energy prices down.

And some of that energy is as clean as the fresh water in the dams that produce the hydropower (although coal is certainly part of the mix).

Miners will move to the cheapest energy source, sometimes on a dime. It's as simple as packing some crates of computers and shipping them elsewhere and plugging in some cables. As renewables and hydro continue their inexorable path to undermining the price of dirty energy like coal, so we will see a continual greening of mining energy infrastructure. This was already in evidence in late 2021 as new green mining ventures started up. *Forbes* magazine covered the green crypto-mining gold rush in its August 13th edition, covering well-funded new ventures like Riot, Scrubgrass and HODL Ranch.

Beyond even the economic certainty of this is the matter of governance. Environmental impact sensitivities are now a staple of company governance, under the rubric of what is called SGI – Sustainable Governance Indicators. Investors, employers, activists and regulators demand it. And given the brouhaha around crypto-mining, the matter now has sharp edges. From individual initiatives like the green crypto-mining project called Seetee (set up by Norwegian billionaire Kjell Inge Røkke) to payment company Square's $10m Bitcoin 'Clean Energy Investment Initiative', pressure has been building. 2021 saw the announcement of the Crypto Climate Accord (CCA), inspired by the Paris Agreement, in which crypto stakeholders have pledged to make this new industry green by 2025.

A tad optimistic? Perhaps, but the path has been laid.

And then there is this – the chips used to power mining (currently a generation of circuitry woefully named 'ASIC') will continue to become more and more energy-efficient (and fast), as they have done without pause since the 1970s. This is a certainty in the competitive and breakneck world of chip and circuit design.

There is a tautological case to be made for balancing the Earth's energy capacity against the many claims of its inhabitants. In the here and now the energy expended on BTC is certainly a concern. But like much else in the march of humankind, it is a concern with multiple paths to mitigation. Yes, Bitcoin transaction usage in the future will certainly increase, adding to the energy load we see today. But a simple linear projection of today's numbers into the future is certain to meet a sticky end, much like the population projections of the Club of Rome in the 1950s – a tale of very smart people getting it embarrassingly wrong (according to those projections we all should have died of starvation and war long ago). Innovation has a way of sideswiping simple projections.

Which leads us to the most important question. Is the energy being expended now (and in the future) worth it, even if it is green? What is the utility of all of this for all of us, and is it worth the power consumption?

There has been much written about the comparison of Bitcoin energy usage to that of other financial services. Some of it, it is fair to say, suffers from shallow analysis. For instance, the energy used in a single Bitcoin transaction has been widely and unfavourably compared to the energy used in a single Visa transaction, forgetting that a credit card transaction is a tiny slice of a much bigger monetary system. Apples and octopuses.

What is that bigger monetary system? Banks and their mainframes, credit cards, debit clearing settlement infrastructures, POS machines, ATMs, notes and coins, central banks, the Swift Network, retail tills. And hundreds of thousands of people to run, guard, count, monitor and regulate all of it. The list is endless.

The energy usage is probably not calculable, especially when you factor in, as commentators have suggested, the armies that defend the governments that safeguard their national currencies and financial systems. A heavily trafficked article by Alex Gladstein in April 2021 entitled 'The Hidden Costs of the Petrodollar' makes the case that any honest appraisal of the dollar carbon footprint has to include the cost of protecting the dollar reserve standard on the global stage. All of this is the lumbering dinosaur to which crypto finance should be compared when considering energy use and carbon footprint.

An unfair comparison? No. Bitcoin and Ethereum and DeFi and the greater crypto-financial family to which they belong represent an entire, fully formed end–end monetary system, running at a vanishing fraction of the energy, people and monetary cost of the traditional global system, and competing robustly in all nooks and crannies of the old system.

Safer, fairer, faster, simpler.

This is indeed the strongest argument against the anti-mining lobby. Energy is being used for crypto. A lot. It was used to deploy a global Internet. And now it is being used to level the financial playing field for all.

Is it worth the energy expended?

Indubitably.

CHAPTER 21

Who will benefit, who will get hurt?

O n June 18th, 2021 a DeFi liquidity project from Iron Finance experienced the crypto equivalent of a bank run, with its TITAN token dropping from over $60 to zero in a few hours. A complete wipe-out. The project used a new sort of algorithmic stablecoin called IRON, which took deposits of IRON/ TITAN pairs to build a liquidity pool. Details are not relevant here – what is relevant is the sudden loss of confidence and the speed of TITAN's price crash. The lack of an FDIC-style insurance left every single liquidity provider 'rekt' (crypto slang for wiped out), including the well-known investor Mark Cuban. It was a shocking event, a complete freefall, unprecedented in DeFi. Over the next few hours rumours and counter-rumours swirled as to whether this was a 'rug-pull', meaning that the project developers drained the account and ran off with the swag, or whether something less felonious had occurred. The latter seems to have been the case. There was a loss of confidence and the algorithmic brakes failed.

We'll come back to this story presently, but let's move on to the larger narrative that is sometimes heard around the edges and occasionally in the heart of DeFi commentary. It is that the entire development of this new set of services is a good guys/bad guys story. It goes like this: the financial institutions of the world are a shadowy cabal that have for too long used their size, leverage, contacts, systems, knowledge and access to political power to build impenetrable structures of wealth creation for the elite, all unwittingly fuelled by us, the common citizens, who are forced to consume their services. Now we the people are going to storm the ramparts and take our power back.

As silly as this sounds, as though drawn from some revolutionary political manifesto, it is indeed the view of many within DeFi whose zealotry is on loud display, even as many others with cooler heads and more realistic goals labour quietly alongside them.

The truth of course, as in all things, is that the spectrum of motives and means is never simple, as much in TradFi as in DeFi. There are good people and bad people all over the place, on both sides of the fence, as well as systems that do not function in ways that they were intended. On the other hand, this new approach to building a world of decentralised finance for all is a fundamental shift, and there will be winners and losers, and some of it will not always be fair.

So who wins, who loses, who gets hurt and who gets happy?

Is it the end of banks? Not in their entirety, of course. But they will not look the same in the years to come. Their brands and relationships and capital pools are wide and deep moats that will protect them against invaders while they carefully decide how and when to woo some of the foreign tribes and their new fancy weapons. But it will be the end of an era of banking and financial institutions, where the asymmetry of information and choice and access was tilted towards the institution and not the customer. That will not hold for much longer.

So let's make some projections. Let's start with who loses.

This one is easy. It is the middlemen, that layer of expertise, escrow and trusted hand-holding that sits between any two parties in an exchange, except for direct private individual exchange. So we have:

- Banks and card companies sitting between a consumer and payment for services or goods.
- Sales agents sitting between companies and raw material purchase.
- Real estate agents sitting between buying and selling parties.
- Brokers sitting in front of institutions like exchanges or insurance companies, handling customer interface and order details, subsequently handing off to order executors.
- Agents and managers acting on behalf of talent.
- Deposits and loans, where the bank acts as the aggregation party, loan-writer and value custodian.
- Commission-based sellers and resellers of all manner of goods.

This list is a small subset of a long list of commercial rent-seekers standing in the middle of transactions. And often there are multiple layers of intermediaries that are engaged, each one providing a sub-service, such as banks that trade stocks for customers, and must deal with exchanges and depositories and others to complete the process.

It would be tempting to say that all of these hand-holders, order-takers and intermediaries are under threat, but that is unlikely to be true, at least in the short to medium term. The entire principle underlying DeFi is the encoding of contractual terms into a deterministic programming language whose logic is open to all, and which is triggered by events in the real world – an entity wishing to make a withdrawal or an interest rate boundary crossed or a date arrived.

But not everything can be reduced to a contract. We have run into this a few times in the preceding pages – human expertise and empathy will always be invaluable in matters of exchange and communication, and irreducible to code, even under the onslaught of AI. So the losers will be the low-hanging fruit first. The fat in the system will be gradually sliced away, the fat that ends up as marbled lobbies and executive perks and outsize salaries and shareholder dividends.

Who will decide to slice this fat away? Not the institutions. At least not voluntarily – that fat comprises some of their profits. But they will be forced to do so as the more technologically sophisticated of their customers simply leave their long-standing banking relationships and entrust their money to DeFi protocols that are providing better, cheaper, faster and more financially beneficial services. This has obviously started already. We have referenced projects with billions locked up in liquidity pools, billions loaned, billions traded. This is just a trickle. But growing. The banks and other financial institutions can surely see where this leads. It leads to simpler and easier interfaces to DeFi, attracting customers who may not be as technology-dextrous – maybe even some smart marketing-savvy middlemen from the world of fintech. And then the customers leaving TradFi turn from a trickle into a flood. And so the impetus will come not from old institutions wishing to offer better new services. It will be a defensive move: how does an old-world bank stop the bleeding? By joining them, not beating them.

But even if the banks do this (and there is already a bunch of banks sniffing around, starting to offer services here and there, including Sygnum in Switzerland and KBank in Korea, not to mention fintechs, for whom this is an obvious next move), there will be casualties along the way. Financial institutions move slowly and carefully, their hands tied by regulation and risk-aversion. Some will certainly not be able to move at the speed required, and will end up launching DeFi services when they are already obsolete. Others will run afoul of regulators (DeFi is still largely unregulated, as we have seen) and some will try to roll their own, a strategy almost certain to fail, given unmemorable previous experiences of banks trying to innovate with other fast and new technologies.

It is more likely that financial institutions will pursue a strategy of acquisition if they can, running both TradFi and DeFi in parallel, and watching to see how the wind blows. The only certainty is that capital will continue to flow out of TradFi into DeFi, and once that quantum is large enough, collateral damage will appear – lower profits, share price pressure, lost jobs.

More damaging will be the assault on the brokerage layer of commerce. Across insurance and other industries, brokers have played a role of translating human requirements into action and sometimes shepherding complex transaction processes to closure, like in the sale of a house. With the rise of smart contracts and oracles, the entire sector of broker interfaces will be under threat. The purchase details (or 'order'), accompanying documentation, workflow, seller offer, payment, clearing and settlement can now be captured in a single contract and implemented on a blockchain. This will be, in some cases, a complex business process requiring excruciating analysis, wherein inputs and outputs and exception handling have to be teased apart in fine-grained detail, and then mapped to code. But as we have said previously, that is an engineering problem, nothing more.

While much of the fizz and pop of crypto has been around the creation of new monetary and financial economies, there are many other industries that will look to blockchain to provide more efficient solutions to complex multi-variate processes, like supply chains. And here we run headlong into a hard fact. It is that most projects that seek to codify a process do not require a blockchain. They require good old centralised computing. There are only a few reasons to use a blockchain – do you want your application to be tamper-proof, mathematically secure, auditable for all time, open, permissionless and trustless? Most people would answer yes to most of these questions. But when pressed about open and per-missionless and trustless, you will find resistance. In those cases a central database, a suite of programs and some off-the-shelf encryption will do. But such is the hype around blockchain that the world is sure to see these solutions being applied to middleman disintermediation, when a 'TradTech' solution would have been cheaper and more efficient.

All of this points the way to another set of losers – not TradFi and not the users of DeFi services, but the many new entrants look-ing to provide innovative services. Here is where Darwinism will be at its most brutal. There are scores of new projects, seemingly every month, each one yelling, 'Better mousetrap, better mousetrap!' We know where this ends: we just have to look back to the hundreds of failed and forgotten crypto projects, or even the explosion of dotcoms earlier this century. Many will disappear, and customers will start to coalesce around a bunch of them, and then just a few of them. But there is a long road between now and then.

When it comes to winners, we can see more clearly. DeFi's entire *raison d'être* is to build a better financial services industry. Which is to give participants, whether they be retail or institu-tional, a richer menu of financial options, easier access to those options, lower costs, higher returns and much more information symmetry between them and us. Anyone touching DeFi is eventually going to be better off than they were under the old regime.

Except ... Iron Finance and the TITAN collapse.

Users of DeFi may one day all emerge as winners, may one day look back and say, remember the terrible old days when we had to apply for accounts, pay all sorts of inexplicable fees and defer to the wisdom of closed institutions. But at least for now, there are going to be some losers among us, like the hapless holders of the TITAN token, and other courageous and perhaps foolish souls who wander into this space before it has settled into adulthood.

There is one last group for whom the winner/loser future is not yet clear, and that is the nation state. Most central banks are now experimenting with Central Bank Digital Currency, CBDC. Its advantages are well understood – real-time gross settlement is a very big pot of gold for national governance. The velocity of money and spend is a fantastic proxy for economic health, and estimates of an order of magnitude increase in velocity via CBDCs are not lost on governments. It will only be a matter of time until CBDCs are standard arrows in the government quiver; we will dig deeper in our next chapter. Government-controlled cryptocurrency will be a clear win for governments that get this right, but a clear competitive loss for those that don't.

But what of cryptocurrencies and DeFi services outside of government purview? This is a terrifying prospect for central banks. A government cannot properly budget and plan national fiscal and monetary policy unless it can have a 360-degree view of the movement of money and prices though the economy. To say it more brutally, unless they can surveille.

Yes, well, that is the way it has worked for centuries. But there is a groundswell of opposition to this, people who say to the government: what I spend and what financial services I buy are no one's business but my own. I pay my taxes, you build the roads, that's the deal. It is certain that citizens will still be expected to pay taxes on DeFi profits, but many tax authorities in different jurisdictions have yet to codify the rules around this, as they grapple to understand this new financial technology.

This is uncharted territory, and who is the winner and loser of that skirmish will determine where the world of private and public finance, money, politics and governance intersect. We suspect it won't be pretty and the battle will reverberate loudly and for a very long time.

CHAPTER 22

Central banks and stablecoins

Even the thought of delving into the subject of central banks makes the authors antsy. It raises visions of mostly white men in austere suits, at least in the Western world, droning on about repo rates and monetary policy and basis points and economic stimulus. We think: damn, a chapter on central banks – this is the easiest way to lose a reader. But stay with us, because they sit at the top of the totem pole, and their authority and oversight filters down to everything you buy or sell or earn or save. Everything. They are all-powerful and not always benevolent. We need to talk about them, because they will intersect with DeFi.

The stablecoin has been a massively successful invention, conceived and developed entirely within the crypto world. From Tether to USDC to DAI stablecoins and others, they are a foundational element across much of DeFi, where their volatility-proof pricing is used as a solid handrail in multiple projects, from liquidity pools to exchanges, not to mention their ability to reach out to real-world financial institutions on pricing terms which are understood by both parties. The accessibility of a programmable currency with its value rooted to the ground has found wide use throughout DeFi.

It turns out that the top dogs of the world's monetary system, the central banks, have been quietly looking on with what we can only imagine was envy and respect, and they are now reacting. Not by trying to crush this nascent competition from within crypto, but by the age-old reliable technique of copying. There are few countries around the world that are not experimenting with national stablecoins. It is coming, and it has DeFi to thank for the thought leadership.

In order to understand why the stablecoin is now front and centre of most central banks' strategies, we are going to take a short tour through the history and function of central banks, and the reason for their primacy in world affairs.

Among other things, a central bank is the mechanism by which nations and their governments inject or remove liquidity, in the form of money, into or out of the economy. It is a spigot when liquidity is increased, and a suction hose when liquidity is reduced. It should come as no surprise that the former happens more often than the latter, reflecting, perhaps, the rise and fall of nations. Nik Bhatia, whose wonderfully concise book *Layered Money* disassembles the history and operations of central banks, says: 'Throughout the ages, currencies have ceased to exist because of one rudimentary fact: governments are unable to resist the temptation to create free money for themselves.' Meaning that, once a nation has the power to inject liquidity into the economy (i.e. turning on the money printers), abuse often follows. The once-dominant Roman Empire stands as the quintessential example: the currency, called the denarius, which started its life as 98% pure gold during the reign of Augustus Caesar, was debased by successive emperors until it was only 5% pure by the 3rd century CE. It didn't end well for the Romans.

Unlike Bitcoin, DeFi was never directly about the creation of a new cryptocurrency. DeFi is a set of services one layer *above* money, services that put money to work, like lending and borrowing. Any creation of 'cryptocurrency' within DeFi has been a side-effect, such as the governance tokens which have found tradable markets of their own within public crypto-exchanges. Nor was there ever any expectation that specialised DeFi coins for governance or liquidity would slowly and quietly migrate to a general-purpose global money like Bitcoin is doing, with some success. (We note here that we are using 'money' and 'currency' interchangeably, which will attract grumbles from purists. Currency is that which gives money life – a dollar bill is currency, and represents a dollar's-worth of monetary value.)

But let's return to central banks, and their very substantive hold on the economy and – by extrapolation – our lives. We will investigate where the world of the central bank and the world of DeFi are likely to collide.

The historical development of currency was accelerated by reliable units of exchange and value (particularly gold and the more pedestrian silver coins). They ticked what have come to be seen as the critical checkboxes of money – scarcity, portability (at least compared to previous units of exchange), counterfeit resistance, recognisability and divisibility – which gave rise to the banking industry. The most famous of the 'modern' banks was the Medici Bank in Florence, which started in the 14th century. The bank was able to provide something fundamentally important when storing coins and currency for customers: it was the 'bill of exchange', which was an IOU, a notice of debt – a promise to pay the bearer the equivalent physical asset which had previously been deposited. There were always coins in these banks, stored safely in vaults to back up the bills of exchange. You brought your coins, they gave you a bill of exchange in return. Such was the reputation of the Medici Bank that this bill of exchange was accepted far and wide, across Europe and beyond.

The bills of exchange (and later innovations like banknotes) and their corresponding physical precious metal deposits were fundamentally different, connected only by the tether of trust. The bills and notes were promises to pay or acknowledgement of debt, and the gold was the actual wealth, the physical object of value. Banks operated in this fashion, with occasional lapses, for hundreds of years. Bank promises and debt were backed with real value.

But it was not to last. Myriad political and economic realities put the absolutism of 100% gold-backed bank paper under pressure. Wars, resource shortages, attacks on currencies, price movements in gold and silver, all catalysed experiments with partly or fully abandoning the gold standard. Although other countries had already started to abandon the gold standard earlier, the dominant global currency giant, Great Britain, 'temporarily' abandoned the standard in 1931, to ward off speculative attacks on the value of its currency, only to find that the economy actually improved, so it never went back.

In the US, there was a different view at the time. The government forced citizens to hand over their gold in 1933 in return for cash and other bank paper in order to stop gold outflows after the Depression (not unexpectedly, people were hoarding gold and other valuable resources). Outgoing President Hoover wryly told incoming President Roosevelt: 'We have gold because we cannot trust governments.' But during the 20th century most countries started moving off the 100% gold standard, while still holding considerable gold reserves as a backstop. Finally in 1971, President

Nixon removed the United States' obligation to 'pay the bearer' in gold, and in October 1976 the statutory definition of the dollar had all references to gold removed. Which meant the international monetary system was entirely free-floating, with one currency's value against another now in the hands of market forces, where it still remains.

The move away from gold reserves was a critical shift in the engines of wealth and in the lenses of public perception. For thousands of years, people's trust had lain in physical objects, whose inherent qualities made them trustworthy and usable as money, gold being the longest and deepest trusted. Even the IOUs, the bills of exchange and other bank-issued paper, always had the comfort of gold collateral sitting in a vault. Now, in the fourth quarter of the 20th century, people had moved their trust from gold to their governments. Bank paper was simply trusted because their governments said so: 'Trust us, we will guarantee the value of this bank-issued note.' As we know from Weimar Germany to Zimbabwe to Venezuela, this has not always turned out well for currency-holders.

There is a reason why we have done a quick tour of the history of the gold standard and its demise. It is that one of the most enduring criticisms of the entire cryptocurrency project has been that its value is not backed by anything. We would argue that since gold retreated, this is now also true of the currency in your pocket. It is backed by the good words and the hoped-for good governance of a group of fallible humans who run centralised governments and institutions.

In addition to the story of the gold standard retreat, there is the historical development of co-dependence between banks and business. Bank expansion and standardisation began with the Medici dynasty, migrating from pure citizen depositories to providers of various sorts of debt for different national, business and personal needs, and across greater and greater geographic distances. And then came the rise of institutionalised international trade, mostly via shipping from the 1500s, followed by bourses and exchanges to capitalise companies, including international trading companies like the Dutch East India Company. And so grew the need for banks to provide debt and other financial rope across all sectors of commerce.

All of this entangled the banks more and more tightly into the business of business, and thus into the economic and political health of the country. It was not long before the nation state said, hang on, surely we should be holding the puppet strings here. Banks need to be under our control, including the creation of money and its release into the economy. Not to mention the setting of interest rates that keep lending and borrowing in balance with saving and spending. And not to mention, again, the funding of wars and other excursions, of which the famous US Federal Bonds which underpinned the capital requirements of the Second World War are a recent example.

Hence the rise of the central bank. The Bank of Amsterdam and the Bank of England and the Swedish Riksbank were among the first, in the 17th century. These institutions took control of the business of gold storage and minting of coins, as well as the issuing of debt (meaning the writing of loans) to the commercial banks now under their purview, which could, in turn, sell debt to private industry. And when gold-backing finally breathed its last, central banks were left with two overriding functions, and the tools with which to achieve them. They are: to control inflation (by stabilising prices) and to encourage maximum employment. It is called the 'dual mandate' in the US, but central bank responsibilities are similar in the rest of the world.

That's it. Just two things.

But the tools that they wield in pursuit of these two goals are impressive. They issue debt to their commercial banks, twiddle interest rates on those loans, mint physical money and distribute it, adjust the capital reserve requirements of member banks, buy securities from those banks, and more. All of this in pursuit of expanding or contracting the *money supply* in circulation, in order to perform their dual mandate, which is the most delicate of balancing acts. Which is why you might wonder what all the fuss is about when the Federal Reserve haggles over a quarter of a percent interest rate move.

There is a mountainous body of policies and frameworks and interpretations and laws that describe the details surrounding all of this, as well as governance and voting and economic models, and guidelines as to which data is pertinent and the boundaries of authority and responsibility of these institutions. But that's really it. Central banks create and destroy money. Or a gentler metaphor: they give and take money, our money, according to rules which they alone decide.

Obviously different countries view the role of these institutions very differently. In some, they are a direct arm of government, in others, completely independent institutions, nominally free of government oversight. Although that latter point is never completely true – chairpersons or chancellors or presidents of central banks are always appointed by ruling parties, never elected. So they are, to a greater or lesser extent, under the influence of the government of the day. And when a government needs to fund something 'big', something beyond the amount available in Treasury coffers, like a war or a pandemic response or a national highway system, it may turn to the central bank for guidance and assistance, or even to apply pressure, subtle or otherwise.

If we take the generous view, we can think of central banks as the wise parents of commercial banks that end up dealing with private businesses and private citizens. It has not always been so, as various governments through history have used central banks as political piggy banks rather than economic tools, but it is the best system we have, and central banks have, for the most part, kept an orderly economic house for many countries, although clearly not all.

There are many in the crypto community who do not take the generous view. Part of the DNA of Bitcoin was to be inflation-proof, to sidestep the central bank's ability to debase money via inflation, as observed by Nik Bhatia. And it is difficult to argue with this. But imagining a world without central banks is like imagining a world without governments. The planet is not about to become one big DAO with a single non-inflatable cryptocurrency at its heart, at least not any time soon.

It is core to the orderly operations of the central bank that they are able to see the movement of money in the economy. Why would they be interested in a stablecoin in the first place? This was clear as early as 2016, when a Bank of England manager gave an address at the London School of Economics entitled 'Central Banks and Digital Currencies'. But it was probably Facebook's announcement of its stablecoin effort on June 18th, 2019, called Libra (recently renamed Diem), that raised the ante. It was one thing for some tiny corner of finance to start trading in stablecoins and experimenting with digital liquidity pools and loans; it was entirely another when Facebook, with its nearly three billion customers, waded into the money game. We suspect that the high priests of central banks all over the world were urgently forced into boardrooms to discuss this, and how and when they should respond.

What they would have seen coming their way was the spectre of money seeping through the economy that they would not be able to count or control, and so would be unable to make well-considered rules to fulfil their dual mandate. They could lobby to have non-governmental money aggressively banned, and it is looking like that will be the case in some autocracies like China, but the liberal democracies might have a harder time with this. And of course, there is the May 2021 announcement by El Salvador, making Bitcoin a dual national currency, thereby conferring legitimacy on a digital currency entirely free of central bank control.

Central banks will need to meet this challenge by competing, and it is clear that the most forward-thinking of them understand this – there were over 80 central banks at various stages of CBDC development at the time of writing. The US is developing Fedcoin (this is the presumptive name from the US Federal Reserve), determined to regain control of the digital currency narrative. It would be a defensive move, and a Fedcoin might well be accepted happily into the crypto playground, notwithstanding the fact that it is unlikely ever to be permissionless or decentralised. A further reason to use stablecoin as defence would be to stay abreast or ahead of countries that are planning governmental stablecoins.

It is no surprise who is ahead in this race. It is China, already testing their stablecoin, the DCEP (the digital yuan) in the market. One can surmise that their goal is partly driven by surveillance rather than citizen privacy, but as mentioned previously, the first country to market with high-velocity programmable digital money gets a huge economic boost.

And then there are the offensive reasons. The removal of clearing and settlement from the economy? That has near-erotic connotations for a central bank, because it would speed up the velocity of a dollar (or any other currency) by two orders of magnitude, potentially supercharging the economy.

On June 22nd, 2021 the Swiss-based Bank for International Settlements (BIS), known as the central bank to global central banks, greenlit, with barely suppressed urgency, the development of CBDCs globally – although it recommended that ID would be required to use currency. Thus setting up the basic philosophical difference between open and closed currencies. Pointedly, Benoît Cœuré of the BIS said of big tech-created money: 'That is a place where you don't want to be, where governments don't want to be', describing it as a loss of control of sovereign money. We suspect he was talking about Facebook's stablecoin Diem.

And more ominously for commercial banks, a central bank with a stablecoin would be able to offer its own DeFi services (perhaps in collaboration with the projects discussed in this book), completely disintermediating the banks and going direct to private citizens with digital cash and perhaps direct to private industry with digital loans. Banks are currently agents of the central banks, they do their bidding and compete with other banks on branding and customer support and product innovation. With no need for clearing and settlement, and instantaneous safe payment and direct smart contract-driven access to lending and borrowing, central banks may start to compete with their member banks.

For a banker this is, perhaps, the most frightening scenario of all.

CHAPTER 23

The future

There were a number of things that became clear while writing this book. The authors, who both have had fairly broad exposure to cryptography, finance and technology, were struck by how few people had heard of DeFi, even within the financial services industry. Everyone had heard about Bitcoin, most had heard about Ethereum, most had heard about blockchains, fewer had any idea that Ethereum was differentiated by its smart contract capability. Where people had heard of DeFi, it was, oh yeah, I think I saw an article about that somewhere.

The suite of applications loosely collected under the umbrella of DeFi have assembled themselves in a tiny sliver of time, most of them since 2017. There have been no real marketing efforts to enlist support or capital from the person on the street; most of the creators and developers have been heads-down in coding, where they most like to be, far from the grubby business of PR and marketing. A few journalists like Laura Shin have gone spelunking and come away with a small library of important stories for news magazines like *Forbes* (and her own newsletter), and a few others, especially podcasters, have poked their noses in and sniffed about. Most of the news, and so most of the public's exposure has been around

Bitcoin, Elon Musk, mining energy usage and the $69m Beeple NFT. Compound? Yearn? Chainlink? It is fair to say that no one has heard of them, outside a tiny elite core, and perhaps they are spoken about in whispers in back rooms of a few financial institutions that are quietly and anxiously looking to the horizon.

It is our firm position that we are on the edge of something transformative here, at least as transformative as the other 'big' new tech ecosystems since the 1970s that have hitched their wagons to some combination of microprocessors, software and the Internet. DeFi's anonymity is something of a riddle; perhaps we are too early in the cycle. But even then we are surprised. A cursory dive into some of the projects will immediately expose, to give one example, interest rate returns on deposits that are dramatically higher than anything that is available from TradFi.

Of course there are people who do know about these services and their startlingly attractive offerings, but choose not to invest for one reason or another. We have written about risk, and it certainly lurks. But there are massive risks in TradFi too, as the collapse of global equity, bond, real-estate and other markets in 2009 should memorably remind us. On the other hand, some of the DeFi projects have hardened considerably. No one has lost money on any of the mature products from Compound or Yearn, for example, and many have been making high double-digit returns for a year or two. Or they have found it simpler to take positions on gold or oil DeFi derivatives, rather than having to be an 'accredited' investor on TradFi derivatives exchanges. So why are the people not coming in their hordes? And why are financial institutions not scrambling to purchase or develop these services?

Perhaps, at least for the average citizen, it is just too damn complicated. We have some sympathy there. We have trowelled our way through dozens of DeFi interfaces. Many are reasonably easy to navigate but they struggle to mask underlying complexity, as the examples in this book might have shown. Liquidity pools and mining incentives and synthetic derivatives and AMMs and governance tokens are intrinsically opaque, an entirely new language from an alien planet.

There are two ways to solve this. One is to explain it better, to which one thinks – who in the world of DeFi has the time? The second is to have a skilled intermediary, human or not, which would simply say: give me your money, I will invest it, you won't believe the returns, check out our record. Or, need a loan? Don't care who you are, no problem, it will be in your account in an hour. In other words, much like a financial adviser or even a robo-adviser from the real world. This is a high-skill undertaking. The adviser would require deep skills, including social skills and considerably more expertise than someone hawking basic bank and insurance company products.

DeFi lacks empathy. It is aggressively labyrinthine. It won't spread without an assist. But here is an interesting perspective shared with us by one of the top developers in the DeFi ecosystem. He kind of prefers it this way. It is an inefficient market. Inefficient markets, for those who spot the cracks, are money machines. As soon as the crowds arrive, the inefficiencies get squeezed out. Outsize returns will be harder to make. Yes, he is right. But we imagine a world, perhaps with utopian-coloured lenses, in which all of us are invited to join a level playing field, with really affordable entry tickets. That might be a wise and good thing, an upliftment for all, so rare in the march of technology. Perhaps a little naive, we know.

And then there are the long-anointed gatekeepers, the guardians of our value, the financial institutions and governmental institutions. Some have glimpsed the tsunami which is headed their way. They will try to fight it, of that we are sure. The financial industry's first instinct will be to protect their turf. They will wield regulation and risk as weapons. They will warn and object and alarm. They will lobby their governments, who will certainly give them cover and laws and bannings and policies. And then some little bank somewhere in a small town will start offering lending and deposit services from Aave or Compound or Kava. Some will white-label Yearn or Curve and deliver outsize yields to delighted customers. Some global exchanges will migrate to AMMs and offer DEX services, perhaps in partnership with one of the Swaps – Uni, Sushi, Pancake and Cow. Some mega-insurance company will quietly copy Nexus Mutual or Cover, or better still, will invite Hugh Karp away on a yacht for a weekend to discuss ways to collaborate. Some central bank somewhere will not only start to settle on Ethereum or Bitcoin, as is already rumoured, but will do it publicly.

And then the skittles will fall fast.

POSTSCRIPT

Over the course of our lifetimes we have seen many new transformative technologies take hold at close quarters, changing the lives of billions in a short time span. As these technologies have gained traction, there has always been robust debate around them. The 'best' PC or the 'best' cellular phone, for instance, or some unintended societal or environmental damage that may be lying in wait. These debates have often spilled over into the public square and front pages. Information and misinformation have battled for hearts and minds. Sometimes better ideas have lost out to inferior ones. Sometimes dire warnings come true. And sometimes rose-tinted glasses have turned out, in hindsight, to have been a little fogged up.

But we haven't seen anything like this before. Cult-like followings, personal animosities, narcissism, threats, anger, accusations, lawsuits, false promises of utopia, public shamings, scam artistry, outright felony. Some of our worst instincts on display, ever since Bitcoin suddenly found a market.

Social media rages continuously, like a fire in gusty wind. Every project has its fierce protectors and shills and barkers. And haters and detractors. And, there in the shadows, always a bunch of young coders working quietly late into the night, hoping that their project is the promised land, and worth the tokens that might have been offered to them in lieu of salaries.

Why this level of emotion? It is because this new technology is at the heart of things.

Money.

Everyone with a stake – DeFi developers, banks, users, investors, governments – all are on a heightened state of alert. This project, that of crypto-enabled finance, is at the top of the fear and greed index.

The new enterprise is asking for our money. Should we hand it over? I will buy a new mobile phone, sign up for a new streaming service, try the latest operating system, download an app. But hand over my hard-earned cash? It doesn't get more real than that.

So you're asking me to hand over my money? we ask.

Yes, hand over your money, they will say.

Why?

Because you will get a better deal from us. Much better than you got from the other guys.

How so?

Well, it's quite complicated …

*

DeFi is coming, notwithstanding.

BREAKING NEWS

As this manuscript entered the final lap of preparation in which no more changes could be made, it was suggested by our publisher that a few update pages be reserved and kept empty to the last minute to keep the book as current as possible in the face of blurring changes.

We thought this was a great idea, but we should have known better. Breaking and important news in every area of this industry arrives daily; tsunamic and ardent. New projects rolling over old ones, bright stars and flameouts, hacks, scams, regulatory wars, TradFi/DeFi collaborations, lobbies and counter-lobbies, alliances, vendettas, and even some signs of technology and service maturation.

So let us cherry-pick just a few and resign ourselves to the fact that we are aiming at a moving target.

On June 29th, 2021, Coinbase, one of the world's largest centralised crypto exchanges, announced plans to offer interest on their clients' passive crypto deposits via a product called LEND. At the end of the first week of September, the US Securities and Exchange Commission served papers on Coinbase (which included the threat of a lawsuit), and Coinbase dropped their launch plans after a few days.

The tangled web woven along the way from Coinbase's announcement of LEND to the retraction of the product on September 12th deserves its own chapter, but there is really only one important message here: the cold war between DeFi and regulators has gotten hot.

Gary Gensler of the SEC has made his intentions clear – DeFi, stablecoins and the larger crypto industry is going to be done his way and all of it now sits in his sights, and the agency is acting, starting now. But he also indicated that he had no intention of banning crypto; this matter rather sits in the hands of Congress. The SEC is concerned with consumer and investor protection – other agencies like the IRS and Treasury (and their equivalents around the world) are muscling up too.

Other than the Coinbase affair, we list, in no particular order of importance (they are all important), some items that post-dated our final manuscript:

In October 2021 the White House announced that it was looking, belatedly, for a crypto czar.

Dan Berkovitz, head of the US Commodities Futures Trading Commission, called DeFi a 'bad idea'.

120 banks are setting up Central Bank Digital Currency experiments and initiatives, up 50% from when we started writing.

China has not only banned mining (discussed in the book), but now all crypto-trading and crypto-holding too. The market barely blinked at the news.

A growing cadre of other countries, from the powerful Brazil to the tiny island nation of Tonga, are presenting El Salvador-style crypto-friendly bills to their legislative assemblies.

Société-Générale, one of the world's largest investment companies, announced an arrangement with MakerDAO in which bonds are used as collateral against a DAI loan (while all of the prior items are important, we believe this one to be *really* important – a perfect meeting of TradFi and DeFi).

In October 2021, there was an announcement by none other than the US Federal Deposit Insurance Corporation that they were 'studying' insurance options for crypto-depositors, which would, all things being equal, be a huge shot in the arm for retail investors.

The SEC subpoenaed Circle, the company backing the stablecoin USDC.

George Soros is investing in crypto and has spoken optimistically about DeFi.

This spectrum of powerful DeFi friends to DeFi foes globally is widely dispersed, and the only certainty is continuing contestation. We have already predicted that DeFi cannot be stopped – though it can certainly be slowed, hobbled, insulted and wounded on its way to global acceptance – but only a fool would try and draw a timeline of future events.

In other matters – from the time of writing the NFT chapter to today, a mere few months later, the industry has moved from merely explosive to positively chain-reactive, with hundreds of companies with NFT-fuelled ideas sucking on the venture capital teat and probing the boundaries of what smart contract-secured ownership can do. As the froth of crazy prices for questionable-quality digital artworks starts to recede, the industry is now reimagining the very nature of what it means to 'own' something, both digital and physical, and how malleable that ownership can be, if defined via the infinite flexibility of computer code. It is likely that NFTs are worthy of a book; the single chapter we allocated cannot do justice to so potentially transformative a topic.

We wrote about the $681 million Poly hack, which was resolved when the hacker returned (almost) all of the funds, negotiating to keep some as a bounty for bug discovery. Unsurprisingly, hacks have continued apace, not as startlingly large (yet), but frequent enough to be alarming. This includes Compound (whom we covered in the book), who suffered not one, but two different hacks between August and October 2021.

The matter of energy usage has started to recede from the front pages, as miners go green and low-energy Proof-of-Stake consensus systems start to gain hold. Not to mention the gradual but steady acceptance of DeFi and other crypto-services as the beginning of something real, useful, transformative and better – and therefore worth the energy expended.

Finally, as we extend this update via a second printing in the year of 2022 we see four major trends. The first is the haste with which governments, regulators and legislators worldwide are tabling laws and regulations, ranging across a spectrum from crypto-friendly to crypto-averse. There continues to be no common approach, and we predict that many of these mandates will have unintended consequences including driving innovation and capital across borders.

The second trend, most evident in the US, is the burgeoning political lobby of crypto-enthusiasts. It is predicted that up to 50 million Americans will have some exposure to crypto investments by the end of 2022. This (and the amounts involved) brings fearsome lobbying power to the industry. Enough, potentially, to swing elections.

The third trend concerns crimes and hacks, where a large contingent of white-hat (ethical) hackers have emerged as volunteer policemen to harden DeFi projects. Plus, the transparency of the blockchain has seen some criminals caught as they leave their trails for investigators. We predict that crime will start to flatten as the bad guys realise that traditional finance is perhaps more fertile ground to which to return.

And finally, evidence of institutional acceptance is growing fast. Aave, a lend/borrow DeFi project mentioned in these pages, has already built a centralised institutional version of their original project. This may violate some of the original blockchain advantages, but it does signal a larger acceptance of the field as a whole.

As we close this update, we are certain that we will wake up tomorrow and wish we could insert just a few more. But that would surely be true every day thereafter too.

INDEX